Headcount or Heartcount?

Leading with Empathy in a Metrics Driven World

By

Avisek Dutta

Made with ♥ on the Notion Press Platform

www.notionpress.com

Dedication

To the loves of my life-

My deepest gratitude to my parents, whose steadfast love and endless encouragement have been my greatest blessing. You gave me roots, and you gave me wings.

To my extraordinary wife, my constant source of strength and inspiration. Your love is the quiet force that empowers me, and your belief in me is the greatest gift.

And to my beautiful, wonderfully unpredictable three-year-old daughter. You teach me every day about the power of resilience, the importance of a joyful spirit, and the true meaning of unconditional love. You're my 'why'.

This book is dedicated to all who strive to lead not from a place of authority, but from a place of empathy and genuine human connection. It's for you.

Contents

Acknowledgement

This book would not have been possible without the encouragement, support, and inspiration of many remarkable individuals.

First and foremost, I thank my family for being my anchor and motivation. Your patience, love, and constant encouragement have carried me through long hours and challenging moments.

To my colleagues, mentors, and peers in the professional world – you have shaped my understanding of what people management truly means. The experiences we have shared, the challenges we have tackled, and the growth we have achieved together all served as invaluable inspiration for these pages.

A heartfelt thanks to every leader and team member who allowed me to witness people management at its best and worst. Your real-life lessons have enriched the narrative and reinforced the human side of leadership.

A special acknowledgment to my dear friend Kanishk, whose unwavering inspiration and encouragement fueled my writing journey.

This book is the result of deep reflection, structured thinking, and creative exploration that guided the writing process and helped me bring clarity and depth to each chapter. Every insight shared here has been carefully shaped by my experiences and personal perspective.

Lastly, I acknowledge the countless unsung leaders – those who lead quietly, with empathy, integrity, and purpose. May this book be a tribute to your work and a guide for others walking the same path.

The title 'Headcount or Heartcount' is inspired by a phrase used by Simon Sinek, whose work continues to influence human-centered leadership thinking.

Preface

Writing the preface to this book "Headcount or Heartcount?" is not just a privilege – it's a deeply emotional experience for me. I have known the author since the moment he opened his eyes to the world. I have seen him crawl, stumble, learn, grow, and ultimately blossom into a compassionate, value-driven professional. But more than that, I have seen him become a fine human being and that, to me, matters most.

Through the years, I have quietly watched his journey with the pride of a mentor, the concern of an elder, and the affection of family. I have seen him handle life's ups and downs with quiet strength, never losing sight of his humanity even while chasing professional excellence. It's this rare blend of empathy and effectiveness that forms the soul of this book.

"Headcount or Heartcount?" is not a management textbook. It's a mirror held up to today's corporate world, where people often become numbers, and results sometimes overshadow relationships. Through honest stories, thoughtful observations, and gentle nudges, the author invites us to look beyond spreadsheets and KPIs, and into the hearts of the people we work with every day.

The beauty of this book lies in its simplicity. It doesn't lecture. It shares. It doesn't boast. It reflects. And because it comes from someone who has spent years in the trenches-facing clients, leading teams, making tough calls – it resonates deeply. There is a quiet maturity in these pages, a steady voice that urges leaders to be more than just taskmasters.

What I find especially moving is that this book is also, in some way, a tribute – to every colleague who stayed back late without being asked, to every manager who chose compassion over convenience, and to every leader who put people before policies. These are the unsung heroes of every organization, and this book gives them a voice.

For me personally, reading this manuscript brought back many memories of lessons learned in boardrooms and lunchrooms, of battles fought with both courage and kindness and as I turned each page, I found myself smiling, sometimes pausing, often nodding in quiet agreement.

If you're someone who believes that work is not just about deliverables, but also about dignity – this book is for you.

If you're a manager wondering whether empathy has a place in a performance review – this book is for you.

And if you simply believe that the workplace can be a little more human, a little more heart, then you've found the right companion.

With warmth and deep blessings,

– Gurudas Chakrabarty
Retired General Manager – HRD
Bank of Baroda

Introduction: People Before Processes

"The only real difference between one organization and another is the performance of its people" – Peter F. Drucker

Let that sink in.

Because in a world obsessed with dashboards, deliverables, and deadlines, we often forget the very thing that makes any organization tick – its people.

Walk into any office – whether it's a buzzing startup or a structured enterprise – and you'll find something quietly powerful at play. Not in the strategy decks or performance reviews, but in the hallway conversations, the subtle glances across meeting rooms, the quiet resilience after failure, and the laughter between back-to-back calls. This book is about those moments. The real, raw, unpolished human moments that define leadership – far more than any KPI ever could.

Why This Book and Why Now?

Because we're at a turning point.

Today's workplace is unlike anything we've known before. Hybrid teams, burnout, generational shifts, automation, diversity dialogues, mental health conversations – the rules are changing faster than the manuals can keep up. In this new world, leadership is not about authority; it's about authenticity. It's not about knowing all the answers; it's about creating spaces where the right questions can be asked.

Yet, here's the paradox.

Most managers are still chosen for their technical brilliance, not their ability to manage humans. They are thrown into roles that demand empathy, influence, and self-awareness – with nothing more than an orientation deck and a hope that they'll "figure it out."

This book is for those managers and those aspiring to become one.

It's for the high performer who's been promoted but now feels like a rookie all over again.

It's for the seasoned manager who's balancing spreadsheets and silent suffering in their team.

It's for the team lead who senses disengagement but can't find the words to reconnect.

It's for the individual contributor who leads without a title but with deep intent.

What This Book Will Help You With

This is not a leadership playbook written from a pedestal.

It's a field guide built from real trenches – where deadlines collide with emotions, where growth meets resistance, and where your biggest leadership wins often happen in moments that no one else sees.

Across the chapters, you'll learn how to:

- Build trust that outlasts timelines
- Give feedback without damage
- Lead meetings that people don't dread
- Handle conflict without avoiding or escalating
- Motivate without manipulation
- Retain talent in the face of change

- Mentor without a megaphone
- And most importantly – lead without losing yourself

Every chapter ends with "Leader's Lens" – reflection questions to spark introspection and deepen your growth. You'll also find "In the Moment" case stories – snapshots from real workplace challenges, encouraging you to pause, reflect, and consider: What would you do?

Because theory doesn't change behavior. Reflection does.

A Personal Word Before We Begin

I did not write this book from a safe distance. I wrote it while leading, learning, faltering, and trying again. From giving my first piece of feedback and watching someone shrink to watching a junior teammate blossom simply because someone believed in them. From sleepless nights after tough conversations to quiet pride in building trust brick by brick.

And along the way, I met people who left indelible marks.

Some taught me what great leadership looks like.

Others, painfully, taught me what it doesn't.

But each one reminded me that people management is not about having power over others – it's about the responsibility we hold with others. It's about replacing control with care, certainty with curiosity, and policies with presence.

So, before you dive in, I invite you to reflect on three simple questions:

1. Who's the one manager who shaped your career for the better? What did they do?
2. What kind of leader do you want to be remembered as five years from now?
3. Are you ready to lead not with a title, but with intent?

If you're still reading, I believe the answer is yes.

So, take a breath. Grab a pen. Dog-ear pages. Argue in the margins. Reflect when something resonates. This is your leadership journey – not just to read, but to live.

Let's begin.

Part I

The Essence of People Management

CHAPTER 1

The Heart of a People Manager

"Leadership is much less about what you do, and much more about who you're." – Frances Hesselbein

A Shift in Identity

For most professionals, the formative years of their careers are dedicated to forging credibility. The expectation is to deliver results, navigate complex problems, and garner recognition. Promotions often arrive as accolades for excellence in execution. Then, one pivotal day, a new title is bestowed – "Team Lead" or "Manager" and the landscape of one's professional life fundamentally alters.

You're no longer solely responsible for your individual output; you become accountable for the collective achievements of others. While metrics may still revolve around deadlines and outcomes, your substantive role has transitioned – from delivering results personally to enabling others to achieve theirs.

Stepping into a people manager role is not merely a superficial change in designation; it's a profound metamorphosis of identity. It transcends overseeing tasks or teams; it demands the cultivation of a mindset deeply entrenched in responsibility, empathy, and enduring impact.

As Fumitake Koga and Ichiro Kishimi articulate in "The Courage to Be Disliked" that you don't need to seek recognition but focus on contribution instead. This profound wisdom challenges the conventional quest for external affirmation. True leadership blossoms not from applause, but from purpose-driven contribution.

The authentic transformation lies in relinquishing the need to be the focal point, choosing instead to truly see others – to elevate, empower, and genuinely serve. When you lead with the intention to contribute rather than to impress, you cultivate an environment where trust, growth, and authenticity can flourish.

It's Not About You Anymore

This transformation can be initially unsettling. New managers frequently discover that the very attributes that propelled their success as individual contributors now hold diminished relevance. Technical prowess remains important, but now they must master patience, refine communication, develop coaching acumen, and deepen their emotional intelligence.

Leadership ceases to be about personal victories. It evolves into uplifting others, skillfully navigating interpersonal complexities, and shouldering responsibility for team dynamics. It involves stepping back with grace so that others may step forward.

The sooner a manager embraces this fundamental shift, the more fluid and rewarding their leadership journey becomes.

More than a decade ago, an email landed in my inbox that would permanently alter the trajectory of my professional life. It wasn't ostentatious – just a concise note with the subject line: "Promotion Confirmation – Manager Grade." Yet, to me, it felt as significant as a golden plaque. I recall that moment with vivid clarity. My heart pounded as I reread the words. After years of relentless effort, extended hours, unwavering commitment, and an unyielding focus on results, what I had, in my mind, finally arrived. I was going to be a 'Manager'.

It felt as though the world had formally acknowledged my capabilities. I had consistently been the one to volunteer for daunting tasks, to remain when others had departed, and to deliver beyond what was merely expected. Naturally, I believed that becoming a manager would be a seamless continuation – an amplification of my abilities, a reward for my performance, and perhaps a platform to shine even more brightly.

What I failed to comprehend was that everything was on the cusp of a profound change.

My first day as a manager lacked any ceremony. There were no trumpets, no celebratory banners, and no effusive welcome speeches. Just a calendar invitation: "Team Introduction and First Connect – 11:30 AM." I strode into the meeting room with a measure of confidence, clutching my notepad, a few printed slides, and the innocent conviction that leadership, like task execution, would yield to sheer determination and willpower.

Upon entering, I was met by a spectrum of expressions: curious, cautious, and some, indifferent. Eight faces. Eight distinct personalities. Eight individual narratives of which I knew nothing. I offered a smile, attempting to break the ice, and introduced myself-a little awkwardly, admittedly. Then, I launched into what I perceived was expected: the goals, the expectations, the deliverables. I believed I was being clear, concise, perhaps even inspiring.

But somewhere between my second and third bullet point, I froze.

Suddenly, the words eluded me. My palms grew clammy. My mouth felt dry. The atmosphere in the room seemed to palpably thicken, and I felt utterly exposed. Looking up, I saw impassive faces – some nodding with polite deference, others visibly distracted. A few were engaged in hushed whispers. It was in that stark moment I realized I was no longer the star performer, no longer the one primarily expected to execute.

I was now responsible. For people. Not merely for outcomes.

That instant became my inaugural lesson in management and arguably, the most crucial one:

This role is no longer about me.

Gone were the days of bulldozing through tasks with singular focus. Now, I was tasked with unlocking that potential in others and not just one archetype of person. My team was diverse in every conceivable sense. There was Roshan, possessing immense technical expertise but lacking confidence in client-facing situations. There was Bhawana, brimming with ideas but grappling with effective time management. There was Vinitha, sharp and ambitious, yet resistant to constructive feedback. Each individual arrived with their unique strengths, inherent limitations, distinct motivations, and personal histories.

Tasks I could dispatch in a few hours as an individual contributor now consumed significantly more time – not due to increased complexity, but because my role now involved explaining, coaching, clarifying, and, crucially, listening far more than speaking. I discerned that managing wasn't about replication – it wasn't about fashioning eight replicas of myself.

It was about cultivating a space where eight unique individuals could perform, grow, and develop an unshakeable trust that I had their backs.

I had to learn to unlearn.

My instinct to immediately intervene and rectify things myself had to be consciously suppressed. I had to permit mistakes – not from negligence, but from a place of faith in their learning process. I had to shift from prioritizing speed to cherishing patience; from being the principal problem solver to becoming the astute problem definer; from claiming credit to generously distributing it; from being the protagonist of the story to becoming a supportive guide, often operating behind the scenes.

Over the ensuing months, I began scheduling more dedicated one-on-one conversations. I started posing more questions:

- What truly motivates you?
- What specific challenges are you currently encountering?
- How can I provide more effective support?

The responses were often surprising. It transpired that my perceptions of their needs and their actual, articulated needs were frequently worlds apart.

Gradually, the team dynamic began to transform. Conversations deepened in substance. Trust began to solidify. They started taking genuine ownership of their work. Some even outgrew their roles, advancing to more significant challenges. And nothing, absolutely nothing, could compare to the profound satisfaction of witnessing an individual flourish under your stewardship – to see them achieve their wins, knowing you played a small, yet meaningful, part in making that possible.

That initial year as a manager didn't just impart the mechanics of leadership.

It taught me humility.

It taught me empathy.

And above all, it ingrained in me the truth that leadership is never truly about the leader.

It's about creating the conditions for others to thrive.

Stepping into a managerial role is like being handed a blank canvas, ready for you to paint your leadership style. The choices you make will define the masterpiece you create.

What Makes People Managers Different

Exceptional people managers think beyond mere task oversight. They concentrate on fostering culture, enabling growth, building connections, and understanding motivation. Their daily actions are informed by questions such as:

- What does my team require to succeed today?
- How can I assist this individual in unlocking their latent capabilities?
- Is there absolute clarity regarding expectations and priorities?
- Who on the team needs recognition, guidance, or reassurance at this moment?

A manager who consistently engages with these questions will seldom stray from the path of effective leadership. Because while strategy and systems are undeniably important, it's the people who execute them that ultimately determine success.

Beyond all these considerations, I discovered something far more profound in my journey as a people manager – a quiet truth not typically taught in leadership training modules, yet possessing the power to transform everything: when a manager forges a genuine, personal connection with their team, an almost magical synergy unfolds.

Not the flashy kind of magic involving grand announcements or awards, but the everyday, subtle kind – the kind that manifests in honest conversations, shared laughter, quiet support during challenging days, and the unmistakable sense of trust that empowers people to bring their authentic selves to work.

Early in my career, I observed this pattern. The managers who left a lasting impact on their teams weren't invariably those with the most prestigious degrees or the sharpest analytical acumen. They were the ones who demonstrated authentic care. They remembered birthdays. They checked in when someone seemed out of sorts. They knew the names of spouses and children. They didn't just manage people – they nurtured relationships. And when they spoke, it wasn't perceived as an instruction, but as a genuine dialogue.

Inspired by their example, I made a conscious decision — a simple guiding principle I have adhered to throughout my people management journey: I would strive to cultivate a familial sense of belonging within my team.

Yes, family. Because, upon reflection, we often spend more waking hours with our teams than with our loved ones at home. We share workspaces, deadlines, and sometimes, even aspirations. We navigate highs and lows together — escalations, team celebrations, unsuccessful pitches, promotions, and late-night problem-solving sessions. These are not merely work moments; they are intrinsically life moments.

When I began to foster this familial connection, something fundamental shifted. My interactions became warmer, more authentic. People started opening up — not just about tasks and impediments, but about their aspirations, anxieties, and even personal setbacks. A team member once shared during a one-on-one, "You're the first manager who visited my mother in the hospital after her surgery." That moment resonated deeply with me. Because in that simple act of remembrance, I had made him feel seen — not as a resource, but as a human being.

And that is what fundamentally distinguishes people managers from task managers. We don't just assign; we listen intently. We don't just review; we relate empathetically. We don't just track performance; we cultivate potential.

It's not always an easy path. Sometimes, this emotional investment entails silently shouldering another's burdens. Sometimes it means late nights spent contemplating how to shield a team member from burnout or how to help another regain lost confidence. But every ounce of that effort is profoundly worthwhile. Because when people feel safe, valued, and connected — they don't just work harder; they work with heart.

I've myself been fortunate to witness this kind of leadership firsthand. Dr. Santosh R Nair, a senior colleague during my time at Reliance Life Sciences, embodied this beautifully. He wasn't my direct manager, yet he treated me with the warmth and guidance of an older brother. He'd go beyond his role, offering advice, sharing a laugh, and sometimes even a gentle scolding – always, always from the heart. A decade has passed since we worked together, but his genuine care and heartfelt connection remain, a testament to the enduring impact of a truly compassionate leader.

Throughout all these years, I've worked under numerous managers. But those who truly stood out were not necessarily defined by high ranks or imposing demeanors. They were the ones who led with warmth, humility, and a profound respect for human emotions. They instilled in me a belief in the power of kindness in leadership and I strive daily to embody that example, because ultimately, people will forget the specific project names and the details of business performance reviews. But they will never forget how you made them feel.

Beyond Control: Leadership Through Trust

Many first-time managers fall into a pervasive pitfall: micromanagement. Propelled by a fear of failure or an innate desire to prove their worth, they meticulously scrutinize every task, double-check every detail, and inadvertently foster an environment of tension and dependency. The outcome? Exhaustion, resentment, and a team that ceases to think autonomously.

But the remedy isn't an abandonment of structure; it's the deliberate cultivation of trust.

Trust-based leadership commences with clarity. You articulate a shared vision, align on expectations, and provide the necessary tools and guidance your team requires. And then-perhaps the most challenging part – you step back. Not to disengage, but to empower.

It represents the shift from declaring, "Do it my way," to inquiring, "How would you approach this? What support do you need from me?" That question doesn't just alter the conversation-it transforms the culture. It conveys faith, honors autonomy, and fosters ownership.

As Carol Dweck notes in Mindset, "Managers who believe people can grow and develop tend to create learning organizations where everyone thrives." When you lead with trust, you cultivate a space where individuals take initiative, venture beyond their established comfort zones, and ascend – not because they are being watched, but because they are believed in.

Six Unspoken Roles of a People Manager

Although job descriptions prominently feature managerial duties like resource planning or review meetings, the true essence of leadership resides in the unspoken roles a manager embodies daily.

First, there is the role of the mentor – offering guidance without imposition, encouraging without overshadowing. Then, the coach – someone who listens attentively, asks probing questions, and facilitates individuals in discovering their own solutions.

Next emerges the shield – protecting the team from unnecessary stress, distractions, or organizational crosscurrents. Every team needs a cheerleader – someone who celebrates victories, however modest. At times, a manager must assume the role of the therapist – the one who offers a patient, empathetic ear when someone is grappling with difficulties. And finally, the firefighter – intervening during crises to contain the fallout and restore equilibrium.

No formal training explicitly prepares you for these roles. Yet, they profoundly shape your effectiveness far more than any policy or process ever will.

Not Everyone is Cut Out for It – And That is Okay

It's vital to acknowledge that not everyone thrives in a people management capacity. Some professionals derive greater fulfillment from deep expertise and individual contribution than from managing others. This is not indicative of failure – it's a testament to self-awareness.

People leadership carries a significant emotional freight. It necessitates empathy, patience, and the capacity to remain composed even when others are not. It also involves accepting that your impact is now indirect. You're no longer the star performer – you're the catalyst for creating stars.

If you're not prepared for that trade-off, pursuing excellence as an individual contributor is a more authentic path. But for those intrinsically drawn to this leadership journey, the rewards – emotional, intellectual, and professional – are both deep and enduring.

I am reminded of a dear friend from my tenure at Reliance Life Sciences – someone for whom I hold profound respect to this day, Mahendra Chavan. He was, in every sense of the word, brilliant. A veritable fount of domain expertise, a sharp, analytical thinker, and a genuinely good human being. Colleagues frequently sought his counsel for solutions that eluded even the most astute minds. His clarity of thought, calm demeanor, and exceptional problem-solving abilities rendered him an invaluable asset to every team he joined.

Naturally, many presumed that someone of Mahendra's caliber would make an outstanding people manager. After all, wasn't that the next logical progression? Promotions came his way, organizational pathways steered him toward managerial responsibilities, and several peers encouraged him to "take charge" of a team. But Mahendra consistently, politely declined.

Not due to a lack of skills, but because he possessed something even more valuable – profound self-awareness.

He understood himself deeply. He knew the wellspring of his energy – working independently, immersing himself in complex problems, and innovating within his specialized domain. He was equally cognizant of what drained him – managing team dynamics, navigating interpersonal conflicts, coaching, mentoring, and being directly responsible for the career trajectories of others. It wasn't a lack of value for people; he simply recognized that his core strength lay in being a stellar individual contributor. And he embraced this path with unassuming confidence.

Over time, Mahendra did not stagnate; indeed, he flourished. He expanded his expertise laterally, leading critical initiatives and becoming the undisputed go-to expert in his field. Organizations recognized his contributions and rewarded him commensurately. He might not have had a team reporting to him, but he commanded the respect and admiration of everyone around him including senior leaders.

The most admirable aspect was Mahendra's unwavering refusal to succumb to societal pressures or conventional definitions of success. He defined success on his own terms.

His story has remained with me over the years, serving as a potent reminder: leadership is not a one-size-fits-all paradigm. While some find profound joy in leading people, others find it in mastering their craft. Both paths are equally valuable. What truly matters is understanding your own strengths, inclinations, and what genuinely brings you fulfillment.

Presence Matters More Than Power

Many managers operate under the assumption that their title automatically confers influence. But titles merely establish formal authority. Genuine influence, however, arises from presence.

Presence signifies being accessible, attentive, and authentic. It means showing up not just physically, but emotionally – especially when someone is feeling stuck, frustrated, or lacking confidence.

When a manager is genuinely present, the team doesn't just follow instructions – they trust. And with trust, every aspect of leadership becomes more fluid-feedback, conflict resolution, and even performance correction.

One of the leaders I deeply admire is Ramanarayana Parhi, and I will likely continue to speak of him in subsequent chapters. He wasn't just a leader; he was a presence-calm, composed, deeply humane, and profoundly grounded.

Despite being the Chief Information Officer (CIO), a role many associate with closed doors, tightly packed schedules, and guarded interactions, Ram was entirely different. He was the kind of individual who remembered not only the names of his most senior team members but also those of trainees and even the pantry assistant who served tea. His memory wasn't merely photographic – it was empathetic. He remembered because he genuinely cared.

I recall one particular instance that left an indelible imprint on me. We were in a high-pressure leadership review, a room filled with tense faces and the clock ticking relentlessly. Ram walked in, smiled, and, as was his custom, took a moment to greet everyone individually. But before the meeting commenced, he turned to a Team Leader who appeared visibly nervous. Ram, however, simply put him at ease by inquiring about his child's school exam scheduled for the following week. That is the kind of memory he possessed – a memory of the heart.

I once mustered the courage to ask him, "Ram Sir, how do you manage to stay so grounded when your schedule is so overwhelming and your responsibilities so immense?" He looked at me, smiled gently, and imparted a piece of wisdom I will carry for life: "If people feel respected, they'll give you, their best. If they feel ignored, they'll give you just enough."

That single line encapsulated the entire philosophy of leadership he embodied. His meetings didn't conclude when the discussion points were exhausted – their impact lingered in the hearts of those who attended. People walked away not just with tasks and deadlines, but with a sense of being seen, heard, and valued.

Long after he had departed the room, his presence remained. Not because of his power, but because of his presence.

Defining Your Own Leadership Style

There is no definitive template for being an exceptional people manager. Your style will inevitably reflect your personality, values, and accumulated experiences. What truly matters is intentionality.

Ask yourself:

- What kind of leader do I aspire to be remembered as?
- Do I lead primarily through fear or through inspiration?
- Am I genuinely accessible to my team beyond the scope of work instructions?
- Do I empower, or do I tend to control?

Leadership is not a static trait – it's an evolutionary journey. What is paramount is your willingness to grow, not by chasing a predefined mold, but by nurturing a style that is both authentic to you and impactful for your team. You don't need to undertake a complete overhaul overnight or become someone you're not to lead effectively. Instead, focus on steady, intentional growth.

As James Clear insightfully states in Atomic Habits, "Every action you take is a vote for the type of person you wish to become." It's these small, consistent shifts, grounded in your identity, that forge meaningful, lasting transformation. When you harmonize your leadership behaviors with your intrinsic values, those incremental adjustments compound over time, shaping not only how you lead, but how others experience your leadership.

I recall one incident that happened a year ago. There was a partial ramp-down going on in one of my projects. The air in the office had thickened with an unspoken tension following the partial ramp-down. While most of our associates, through diligent effort and a dash of luck, found new homes within other accounts, one individual remained adrift. He didn't secure a new project and, in an unfortunate turn of events, had to depart the organization.

In the weeks that followed, a peculiar form of communication began. My phone buzzed persistently with messages from him – not direct complaints, but a steady stream of subtle, often pointed, videos and memes depicting dysfunctional workplaces and quintessential examples of poor management. Each one felt like a whispered accusation, a digital mirror held up to my own leadership, indirectly hinting that perhaps I, too, was falling short.

It would have been the easy, even expected, path to simply block him, to silence the discomfort and move on, as many of my colleagues advised. There was a strong, rational argument for it – a 'headcount' approach to managing a perceived nuisance. But something within me, a stubborn belief in the 'heartcount' over the 'headcount,' urged me to listen deeper. Despite the discomfort, and the silent judgment of some, I chose not to shut down. I kept replying, acknowledging his messages, and even finding genuine elements to appreciate in some of the content he shared. It was my way of signaling that I was truly listening, truly seeing him, acknowledging his pain and frustration without validating the implied critique.

Then came his birthday. I sent him a simple note wishing him well, devoid of any mention of work or the past. The response was immediate and stark in its sincerity: 'Thank you Sir.' In those two words, a dam broke. It was a moment of raw, unadulterated shock and gratitude. That was the last message of its kind I ever received from him. He never sent another 'poor management' meme. The stream of subtle criticisms ceased. What began as a contentious post-departure dynamic transformed into quiet respect, simply because I chose connection over convenience, empathy over efficiency. It was a powerful reminder that sometimes, the most profound leadership impact comes not from strategic moves, but from a simple act of human kindness.

In the end, true leadership is less about control and more about connection – to your purpose, your people, and your principles.

It Starts With Heart

At its very core, people management is not about tools, trackers, or dashboards. It's about the bedrock of human connection. It's about uplifting others, not merely leading them.

Show up with clarity. Lead with empathy. Listen with intent. And remember that the most impactful managers are not those who are feared, but those who are trusted and remembered – for how they made people feel.

> *"Leadership is measured by Heart-Count of Followers and never by Head-Count of Followers"* – Roger Simpson

CHAPTER 2

HRM Beyond HRD – The Frontline Reality

"Treat employees like they make a difference, and they will"
– Jim Goodnight

Looking Beyond the HR Department

When the term Human Resource Management (HRM) arises, most individuals instinctively envision the Human Resources department (HRD) – the architects of recruitment, payroll, policy frameworks, appraisal systems, and compliance mandates. This association is natural, as these represent the overt, tangible functions of HR.

Yet, in its truest sense, the tendrils of HRM extend far more pervasively. The authentic human resource experience isn't forged within the confines of HR cubicles or through standardized circulars. It's meticulously constructed in the crucible of team meetings, daily interpersonal exchanges, one-on-one dialogues, and the observable behaviors of managers. It's less about codified policies and more about the intrinsic feelings it evokes within each team member.

Every individual's perception of the organization is more profoundly shaped by their immediate manager than by the collective efforts of the HR team. This unequivocally indicates that, whether you possess the formal title or not, if you guide a team, you're, in essence, an active practitioner of HRM – each and every day.

The Three Layers of HRM

Academics frequently delineate HRM across three distinct strata: what is intended, what is implemented, and what is experienced.

The initial stratum, intended HRM, represents the blueprint architected by HR. This encompasses performance frameworks, organizational policies, recognition programs, and defined career progression pathways. The second, implemented HRM, is the translation of these frameworks into tangible managerial action and practice. The final, and arguably most critical layer, experienced HRM, encapsulates how employees internalize and perceive these actions and the overarching workplace environment.

Even the most meticulously crafted policies are destined for inadequacy if managers fail to implement them with requisite care and transparent clarity. Conversely, even standard or average policies can foster a sense of empowerment when leaders infuse their execution with empathy, consistency, and inherent fairness.

Your Influence as a Manager Is Greater Than You Think

Reflect upon your own career trajectory. Was it the HR policy handbook that truly ignited your motivation, or was it the manner in which your manager treated you? When a superior exercised patience during your developmental phase, when they offered unwavering support in the wake of an error, or when they demonstrated genuine interest in your professional aspirations – that was HRM manifesting in its most potent and resonant form.

As a manager, your tone, your discernment of timing, and the trust you cultivate carry far greater weight than formal processes alone. You're the embodiment of the organization to your team. Their comprehensive experience of the company is often a direct reflection of their interactions and relationship with you.

This considerable responsibility may feel daunting at times, but it concurrently signifies that you possess the profound capacity to sculpt careers and cultivate vibrant cultures from their very foundations.

One of the most impactful statements I've encountered in leadership literature emanates from Satya Nadella, CEO of Microsoft. In his paradigm-shifting memoir Hit Refresh, he asserts:

"Empathy makes you a better innovator and a better leader."

At first blush, this may sound merely poetic – perhaps even idealistic. Delve deeper, however, and you'll unearth it as one of the most profoundly strategic linchpins for effective people management in the contemporary era.

Traditionally, empathy was often relegated to the periphery under the 'soft skills' umbrella, viewed as an optional attribute to be practiced predominantly by HR professionals or counselors. Today, however, empathy is rapidly emerging as an indispensable leadership competency-one that fundamentally defines how leaders connect, create, and catalyze meaningful change.

In my own journey as a people manager, I've witnessed this truth firsthand. The most resilient teams are not necessarily those shielded from all forms of stress, but rather those whose members feel a profound sense of psychological safety – safe enough to articulate their fears, acknowledge mistakes, and proactively seek assistance. And that bedrock of safety is invariably rooted in empathy – not merely in policies.

When a manager consciously pauses to inquire, "What's genuinely transpiring with this individual?" instead of prematurely leaping to judgment, that single, thoughtful question can alter the trajectory of an entire conversation – or, indeed, a career. It's empathy that enables us to discern when underperformance stems not from incompetence, but from being overwhelmed. It's empathy that reminds us to celebrate discreetly with an introverted team member who finds public applause uncomfortable. It's empathy that informs us when someone requires a gentle nudge – and when they simply need to be heard and understood.

Empathy doesn't necessitate becoming emotionally enmeshed in every challenge your team confronts. Rather, it means acknowledging their intrinsic humanity and responding with heightened awareness and deliberate intention.

And the brilliance of Nadella's insight lies precisely here: Empathy not only fortifies your ability to lead people – it concurrently sharpens your capacity to innovate.

When you comprehend your people on a deeper level, you don't just manage more effectively. You begin to architect superior solutions, implement more intelligent processes, and foster healthier organizational cultures. You transition from transcending superficial symptom management to addressing fundamental root causes. You learn to anticipate resistance, pre-empt burnout, and inspire enduring loyalty.

I've observed managers with comparatively lesser technical expertise significantly outperform their counterparts, simply because their understanding of people was more profound. They didn't passively await HR intervention to resolve team tensions – they possessed the acuity to sense nascent conflict and address it informally. They didn't defer to policy changes to uplift morale – they elevated spirits through subtle yet significant gestures: an impromptu coffee chat, a thoughtfully worded thank-you message, a well-timed, supportive phone call.

These are not grandiose actions. But they are intrinsically human gestures, generating resonant ripple effects that no HR policy, however well-intentioned, could ever replicate.

So, as we deliberate on redefining HRM for the modern world, it's imperative that we retrieve empathy from the "soft skills" repository and position it front and center – as a leadership superpower, a strategic lens, and an undeniable catalyst for organizational transformation.

Real HRM Happens in Everyday Actions

Authentic HRM doesn't invariably present with dramatic flair. It's embodied by the team leader who remembers an individual's family circumstances and judiciously adjusts timelines. It's the manager who delivers candid feedback with a finesse that preserves, rather than erodes, confidence. It's the senior colleague who offers a simple, heartfelt "thank you" when such courtesies are often overlooked in the rush of daily activities.

Engagement, retention, development, and morale – these critical indicators do not fluctuate based on annual town halls or grand pronouncements. They ebb and flow in direct correlation with the cumulative sum of interactions and experiences occurring between the commencement of Monday morning and the close of Friday evening.

Seemingly small things such as how you handle a leave request, your response to a mistake, or the manner in which you include someone in a crucial meeting, eloquently communicate to your team whether they are perceived merely as employees or as genuinely valued individuals.

A Tale of Two Teams

Let us envision two teams operating within the same organization. Both have identical access to resources, operate within the same compensation structures, and are governed by the same organizational policies. Yet, one team is flourishing – characterized by robust collaboration, high engagement, and minimal attrition. The other is marked by disengagement, prevalent grievances, and a consistent pattern of departures.

What accounts for this stark difference?

Is it HR? Almost certainly not. The differentiating factor is, invariably, the manager.

One manager integrates HRM as an intrinsic component of their core responsibilities – proactively building trust, offering constructive feedback, recognizing individual strengths, and ensuring their availability. The other manager views such matters as the exclusive domain of the HR department, passively expecting them to handle engagement and morale. Over time, each team responds in kind to these distinct leadership approaches.

This is precisely why frontline leadership is the veritable engine of effective HRM. An organization's culture is not forged in corporate slogans or mission statements, but in the crucible of everyday leadership behaviors.

A Personal Story: The Real Face of HRM

More than a decade ago, I had the distinct privilege of working under an individual who didn't just redefine leadership for me – he recalibrated my understanding of humanity within the professional sphere. His name was Dr. Sunil Chaudhry. While his official title bore no HR designation, he embodied every intrinsic value that human resource management is fundamentally intended to champion. He wasn't merely a senior leader; to many of us, he was a trusted guide, a steadfast protector, a dedicated mentor – and for me, personally, he became akin to a father figure.

At a juncture when I was still actively shaping my comprehension of people management, Dr. Sunil stood apart, not merely because of what he did, but profoundly because of how he did it – with an inherent grace, profound wisdom, and the rare, innate ability to make individuals feel genuinely seen and unequivocally safe. He possessed a remarkable presence; his entry into a room often had a visibly calming effect. He carried himself with an understated dignity, yet never with even a hint of aloofness. Most importantly, he harbored an unwavering, optimistic belief in people.

He lived by a simple yet extraordinarily powerful principle:

"If my team is not growing, I'm failing."

And he meant it with every fiber of his being. He noticed everything – not in a controlling, scrutinizing manner, but with genuine care and attentiveness. He observed how individuals communicated in meetings, whether someone appeared unusually withdrawn on a particular day, if an employee was exhibiting nascent signs of burnout, or if someone was simply yearning for a word of recognition. He perceived nuances that most managers, immersed in their operational duties, often missed. It was as if he possessed an innate emotional radar, perpetually attuned – not because it was a stipulated part of his job, but because it was integral to his very nature.

One of the most potent lessons I gleaned from him unfolded during a period when I had committed a serious error.

It was unintentional. But owing to a misjudgment on my part, I unwittingly transgressed a significant company policy – one that carried tangible consequences and, more critically, attracted the pointed attention of senior stakeholders. As the news of my lapse escalated, I could physically feel the walls closing in around me. I had never before found myself in such a professionally vulnerable predicament. My heart pounded relentlessly. My self-assurance had utterly disintegrated. I braced myself for the anticipated reprimand, for the chilling silence of disapproval, or at worst, for professional isolation.

Instead, Dr. Sunil entered the room, placed a reassuring hand on my shoulder, and in a voice only I could discern, whispered:

"It's not a big deal. I know your intention was 100% in the right place."

In that single, empathetic sentence, he restored everything the preceding 24 hours had stripped away – my dignity, my belief in my own integrity, and my crucial sense of psychological safety. He didn't demand an explanation. He didn't solicit justifications. He had already perceived the underlying truth – not in the error I had made, but in the honorable intention that had guided my actions.

What transpired subsequently was even more remarkable. He took complete ownership of the situation, calmly addressed the concerned stakeholders, and meticulously ensured the matter was resolved without any detriment to my integrity or professional standing within the team. Later that evening, once the proverbial dust had settled, I approached him to express my profound gratitude. He smiled, almost as if he had performed no extraordinary act, and simply said:

"Policy is important. Work is even more important. But people matter more to me."

That wasn't a maxim I had encountered in any HR manual. It wasn't a quote from a management treatise. That was leadership emanating from the soul. That was HRM in its purest, most unadulterated form – not confined to paper, but lived in practice.

It was in that poignant moment I truly understood that human resource management is not merely a function. It's a philosophy. A conscious choice. A deliberate way of showing up for people, not just when they achieve success, but especially when they falter or stumble. Dr. Sunil didn't just manage performance; he actively nurtured growth. He didn't just protect reputations; he painstakingly built resilience.

Years have now passed, and I've collaborated with many other leaders since. Yet, every time I am confronted with a situation that demands compassion, fairness, and courage, I find myself introspectively asking – What would Dr. Sunil do? Because in a world where leaders are often primarily judged by how effectively they manage outputs, he taught me that true leaders are ultimately remembered by how they treat people, especially when no one else is watching.

And perhaps that, in essence, is the real face of HRM.

Practicing HRM as a Manager

You don't require an encyclopedic knowledge of policies to evolve into a people-centric leader. What you do need is to be consistently intentional in your approach.

Commence by engaging in authentic conversations. Strive to understand what genuinely drives your team members, what impediments block their progress, and what truly excites and energizes them. Provide timely, constructive, and considerate feedback. Celebrate progress and effort, not solely final outcomes. Establish clear, unambiguous expectations, and remain flexible enough to adjust them when circumstances necessitate.

When you consistently practice these fundamentals, your team doesn't just meet its goals – they grow, they demonstrate loyalty, and they genuinely thrive.

Changing the Narrative

It's high time we collectively pivot from reflexively stating, "HR should fix this," to proactively asking ourselves, "How am I, as a manager, actively shaping the experience for my team today?"

The most effective managers don't passively await HR initiatives. They proactively cultivate engagement through how they present themselves, how attentively they listen, and how thoughtfully they lead.

Many of us have matured in corporate cultures where a significant portion of responsibility for employee well-being is often unconsciously, almost reflexively, delegated to Human Resources. When morale dips, the default is often to look to HR to organize a team-building event. When confusion arises, the expectation is for HR to disseminate an official clarifying communication. When a crisis erupts, there's a tendency to wait for HR to convene a townhall and "manage the situation."

But over the years, I've come to firmly believe and witness repeatedly that this prevailing mindset is ripe for a fundamental re-evaluation. It's time we cease declaring, "HR should fix this," and instead, begin to consistently ask, "What am I doing, as a manager, to shape my team's experience today?"

The finest people managers don't wait for a policy directive. They don't wait for someone from HR to distribute a survey. They instinctively take ownership. They lean in with unwavering presence, profound empathy, and decisive action.

I learned this lesson indelibly during one of the most challenging professional chapters I've ever had to navigate.

It involved a substantial, high-stakes endeavor engaging over 200 employees. For months, the team had been investing their all-working extended hours, diligently managing deliverables, adeptly navigating stakeholder demands, and coalescing with a quiet resilience that stems only from deeply shared commitment.

And then, one day, with absolutely no prior intimation, the client delivered devastating news: The project was being abruptly terminated. To compound matters, in what I can only surmise was an unfortunate oversight or a grave misjudgment of protocol, the client included the entire 200+ member team in the termination email. The communication was cold, starkly factual, and unequivocally final. There was no trace of empathy. No contextual explanation. No preparatory warning. No transition plan.

Within minutes, panic proliferated like wildfire. My inbox was inundated. My phone rang incessantly. People were understandably terrified. Some were in tears. Many had financial obligations – loans, young children, elderly parents, dependents – and all they could foresee was an abrupt descent into uncertainty.

In that critical moment, I did not possess all the answers. But one thing I knew with absolute clarity:

I could not, and would not, wait for HR.

This wasn't born from a lack of trust in them; I have always held my HR colleagues in high esteem. It was because, in that crucible of crisis, I was the face my team looked to. I was their anchor, their perceived source of stability. So, I stepped up. Not as a fulfillment of a formal requirement, but as a deeply human instinct.

I dedicated the subsequent 48 hours to doing everything within my capacity. I personally connected with numerous individuals – through phone calls, impromptu huddles, video chats, even informal tea breaks. I took it upon myself to reassure, to explain to the best of my ability, and, most importantly, to actively listen.

For some, a few words of comfort sufficed. For others, it involved navigating through palpable fears and intense emotional outpourings. I reminded them that their contributions had been invaluable, that the organization wouldn't abandon them, and that I would leverage every resource at my disposal to ensure their stability and dignity were safeguarded.

But words alone were insufficient. I knocked on every conceivable door. I contacted leaders across various departments. I diligently pursued staffing leads. I called in favors I hadn't utilized in years. And gradually, one by one, with the crucial assistance of my peers from other accounts and the senior leadership team, I began the painstaking process of reallocating team members to new projects, advocating for them with the same fervor I would for my own family.

It was an arduous undertaking. It demanded days of negotiation, considerable back-and-forth communication, and an emotional toll greater than I could have anticipated. But when the dust finally settled, not a single team member was left without a role.

The messages I received afterward – the expressions of relief, the heartfelt gratitude, the silent, appreciative nods in the corridor – I cannot adequately articulate their profound impact on me. One team member sent me a handwritten note that simply read:

"You did not just save our jobs. You restored our faith."

Honestly, however, I didn't undertake those actions for appreciation. I did it because, in that defining moment, I realized something incredibly powerful: People management is not merely a role. It's a profound responsibility.

Being a people leader signifies that you're accountable not just for performance metrics, but for pivotal human moments – especially those for which no one explicitly prepares you.

This experience wasn't solely about managing a crisis. It was about how I consciously chose to show up within that crisis. It was about fundamentally changing the narrative, from passively waiting for HR to assume control, to proactively taking charge with heart and conviction.

That experience irrevocably reshaped me. It taught me that while systems and processes are undeniably critical, nothing can ever replace the power of human presence, individual initiative, and empathy in action.

And if even one person slept more soundly that night because I showed up for them – then to me, that embodies leadership in its truest, most authentic form.

HRM Is in Your Hands

Human Resource Management is not circumscribed by job offers, onboarding packages, or performance rating scales. It breathes within every dialogue between a manager and a team member. It's manifest in the manner feedback is imparted, how recognition is genuinely offered, and how the foundations of trust are painstakingly built and nurtured.

As a people manager, you're not just a constituent part of the organization. You're the organization – in the eyes, hearts, and minds of your team.

> *"Human resources isn't a thing we do. It's the thing that runs our business" – Steve Wynn*

CHAPTER 3

Communication and Connection

"The biggest problem in communication is the illusion that it has taken place." – George Bernard Shaw

Why Communication is the Core of Leadership

Many professionals assume that communication is about speaking clearly or writing a well-worded email. But leadership communication is much more than that. It's not just about words – it's about building understanding, connection, and trust.

As a people manager, your ability to communicate shapes your team's morale, alignment, and willingness to follow you. Communication is the bridge between what you want as a leader and what your team delivers. If that bridge is weak, unclear, or unreliable, everything else – including performance – suffers.

The Many Dimensions of Managerial Communication

To lead effectively, managers must communicate in more than one way. First, there is the basic, transactional communication – giving instructions, setting deadlines, clarifying roles. This is essential, but it's only the surface.

More impactful is the developmental communication – providing feedback, guiding careers, asking reflective questions. Then comes emotional communication – the ability to connect, empathize, and encourage during highs and lows. Finally, there is strategic communication – aligning the team with broader goals and inspiring them to move forward with purpose.

Great leaders don't stick to one type. They move fluently across all of them, depending on the moment and the need.

Listening: The Superpower Managers Underuse

In the world of management, we often talk about vision, strategy, influence, and execution. Yet one of the most powerful tools – one that can turn around morale, rebuild trust, and quietly transform entire teams – is often the most underused: listening.

Not passive hearing. Not waiting for your turn to speak. But intentional, focused, empathetic listening – the kind that makes people feel seen, heard, and valued.

Most people listen to reply. A few listens to truly understand. And therein lies the difference between a manager who manages, and a leader who connects.

Several years ago, I found myself in one of the most complicated people management situations of my career. I had just been assigned to lead a massive project – one that involved over 300 team members spread across different functions. On paper, it looked like a great opportunity. But the moment I stepped in, I knew I was walking into a storm.

The previous leadership had just exited. There had been a sudden restructuring. Communication had been inconsistent, and whispers had filled the vacuum. To make things worse, a salary correction exercise had been carried out before my arrival – but only for a selected few.

The news had trickled out, and unsurprisingly, it triggered resentment and distrust across the team. People were angry. Not just because they did not get the raise – but because they did not understand why they did not. There had been no clarity, no context, and no explanation.

When information is scarce, speculation thrives. And that is exactly what happened.

I did not have the answers. The decision had been made before my time, and I wasn't privy to the selection criteria. But none of that mattered. I was now the face of leadership. And people were looking at me – not just for direction, but for acknowledgment.

So, I did what I always do when the stakes are high and clarity is scarce – I reached out to my guide, Mr. Ramanarayana Parhi.

Ram listened. Patiently. Thoughtfully. As always, he did not rush into action. After I laid out the mess, the lack of information, the tension brewing across the team, he said, "You can't fix this overnight. But you can heal it. Start by listening. Sometimes, people don't want a solution. They want a space to speak, to be heard. Go give them that space."

It sounded deceptively simple. But I trusted him.

The very next morning, I walked into the office by 8:00 AM – earlier than usual. I hadn't prepared a long speech or a PowerPoint. I only had a notebook, a pen, and an open mind.

I started calling team members – not in groups, but one by one. Especially those who I had heard were most upset. I met them in quiet corners, near coffee tables, in vacant meeting rooms and I asked just one thing: "Tell me what's bothering you. I'm here to listen."

Some spoke cautiously. Some broke down. Others were visibly frustrated. Many started their sentences with "I know you're not responsible for this, but..." And I just listened. I did not interrupt. I did not try to explain. I did not offer ready-made solutions.

I just listened. I kept on listening for 15 straight hours. No lunch. No formal breaks. Just a steady stream of unheard voices being given room to speak, to vent, to express.

They talked about more than just pay corrections. They spoke of feeling invisible, of being passed over, of years of effort going unacknowledged. They told me about family pressures, financial strains, and dreams that seemed to keep slipping further away. What they wanted wasn't just a hike – they wanted validation.

It was exhausting. But it was sacred.

That day, something shifted. The people who walked in with crossed arms and furrowed brows left with gentler eyes. Many thanked me. Some simply nodded silently. But all of them realized one thing: "Someone is finally listening."

That evening, as I sat at my desk – mentally and emotionally spent – I knew I hadn't fixed the system. But I had done something equally important: I had restored trust.

Over the following weeks, things began to stabilize. People who were on the verge of leaving decided to stay a little longer. Collaboration improved. Conversations became more open. The bitterness that once hung heavy in the air began to lift.

And it all started not with a speech, not with a policy update – but with presence. With listening.

We often underestimate the power of silence and attention. But when wielded with sincerity, listening becomes leadership. It tells people:

You matter. Your voice matters. I may not have all the answers today, but I care enough to hear you.

In leadership, we are taught to speak well. But the true superpower is to listen well. Because sometimes, just by listening, you create a space where healing begins – where dignity is restored, and where hope finds its way back in.

And if you ask me what I learned most in those 15 hours? It's this: Before people will trust your decisions, they need to trust your intention. And that trust is built not through explanation – but through attention.

The 1:1 Conversation: Your Leadership Mirror

If leadership had a mirror, it would be the one-on-one conversation.

Not the weekly project update. Not the scheduled status sync. But the real 1:1 – the space where masks can drop, voices soften, and people are finally allowed to speak, not just about tasks but about truths. And yet, this tool – so simple, so human, and so powerful – remains one of the most underutilized tools in people management.

A true one-on-one is not a calendar ritual. It's a relationship ritual. It's a commitment from the manager that says, "You matter. Not just your output, but you." It's where career aspirations surface, silent struggles find a voice, feedback is exchanged without fear, and most importantly – trust is built.

In my years of leading and being led, I've seen how regular, genuine 1:1s can become the pulse-check of a healthy team. I've also seen the absence of them become the breeding ground for resentment, disconnection, and eventual attrition.

But perhaps the most profound understanding of the power of 1:1s came from one of the best managers and guides I've ever had the privilege to work under – Abhishek Garg.

Now let me paint the picture honestly – at first glance, Abhishek can come across as intimidating. There is a certain intensity in his demeanor. He's sharp, deeply analytical, and has a laser-focused approach to execution. In fact, many who don't know him well, including people far senior to him, often find themselves a little on edge in his presence. You wouldn't catch him smiling casually in the hallway or indulging in small talk at the corridor.

But here's the thing about Abhishek: once you've had a real 1:1 conversation with him, you realize everything you thought you knew about him was only half the story.

Abhishek is the kind of leader who never misses a 1:1. No matter how packed his schedule is, no matter how intense the week has been, those conversations remain sacred. And it's not about ticking a box. It's about holding space.

From the very first 1:1 I had with him, I noticed something extraordinary. He made it clear that this wasn't just his meeting – it was mine. I could talk about anything – not just the metrics or deliverables. He asked questions that went beyond performance:

"How are you feeling about your work these days?"

"Everything fine with your family?"

"Are you learning enough since I know that is what you prefer the most?"

"Is there something you wish you could tell me but haven't?"

And then, he would just listen. Not the distracted kind of listening that managers sometimes offer between glances at emails or message pings. Abhishek would lean in, and give you the kind of undivided attention that makes you feel like you're the most important person in that moment.

And that is when his real leadership showed up.

The tough exterior? It melted away. What stood in front of you was not a figure of authority, but a mentor, a champion, a coach, and on some days, even a quiet confidante. He did not pretend to have all the answers. But he always made sure that you walked out of the room feeling lighter, stronger, and more supported than when you walked in.

I've seen people walk into those 1:1s with apprehension, and walk out with renewed belief – not just in the system, but in themselves. Because when someone listens to you that intently, it sends a signal deeper than words:

"You matter. Your voice matters."

That is the power of a well-held 1:1.

Something that I can say about Abhishek and that too strongly: "I'm not scared of him. I just respect him too much to disappoint him."

And that, in essence, is the hallmark of great leadership. Not obedience born out of fear, but respect born out of care, presence, and earned trust.

I owe a lot of my people management approach to the example he set. Because watching him lead those conversations taught me that leadership is not about being the loudest voice in the room – it's about creating a room where others find their voice.

So, if you're a manager reading this, let me offer you this reflection:

How are you showing up in your 1:1s? Are they transactional, or transformational? Are they driven by tasks, or fueled by trust?

Because at the end of the day, metrics may define your role – but meaningful conversations will define your impact.

Difficult Conversations: Where Real Leadership Shows Up

There is a saying in leadership circles: "Anyone can lead when things are easy. True leadership is revealed in discomfort." Nowhere is this more evident than in the space of difficult conversations – those moments where empathy and accountability must walk hand in hand.

As people managers, we often find ourselves faced with situations that test not just our communication skills, but our character.

Conversations around underperformance, behavioral concerns, feedback, or conflict resolution are rarely comfortable. But avoiding them only makes things worse – for the employee, for the team, and for the manager's own credibility.

The truth is, how we handle difficult conversations defines us more than how we celebrate success and I learned this lesson not from a book, but from a quiet moment that unfolded a few years ago – a moment that still shapes how I approach people in their most vulnerable phases.

We had recently hired an associate with an impressive background. His resume spoke of accomplishments, awards, and steady growth. During the initial weeks, he delivered well – sharp, responsive, and eager to make a mark. But somewhere around the third month, something shifted.

His performance began to dip. Quality errors started surfacing. Deadlines were missed. His interactions grew distant, and the energy he once carried into meetings was replaced by a visible sense of withdrawal. Naturally, supervisors were getting anxious. His appraisal ratings were beginning to suffer, and murmurs of dissatisfaction started floating through the corridors.

It would have been easy and frankly very common to label the associate as disengaged, lazy, or complacent. A typical performance review might have involved strong warnings, documentation, and corrective plans. But instead of rushing into judgment, we chose to pause. We chose to ask a different question:

"What might be going on beneath the surface?"

So, we decided to sit down with him – not as a disciplinary action, but as a conversation. We intentionally avoided the usual phrases like "performance concerns" or "expectation gaps." Instead, we invited him for a relaxed chat, without formal agendas or timelines.

He entered the room with caution, probably expecting to be reprimanded. But when we gently asked, "How are you doing – truly?" something changed in his demeanor. For a few seconds, he looked unsure. Then his eyes softened.

He told us, haltingly at first, that he had been struggling with his health. There had been a recent medical scare, and while the diagnosis wasn't severe, the fear had been gnawing at him. He hadn't told anyone because he did not want to appear weak or unreliable. But the stress was real. The anxiety had been affecting his focus, his energy, and his confidence.

In that moment, the room transformed. We were no longer managers talking to an employee. We were humans listening to a fellow human in pain.

We immediately told him to take time off if needed, without hesitation. But more than that, one of his supervisors – someone he respected deeply – looked him in the eyes and said something that I believe changed everything:

"You're going to be okay. And even if it takes time, we'll be right here."

That moment wasn't rehearsed. It wasn't strategic. It was real.

Interestingly, he did not take that leave. What he took instead was a renewed sense of belief – in himself, and in the people around him. Slowly, over the next few weeks, his work began to improve. Not dramatically. Not overnight. But consistently. His confidence returned. His tone brightened. And his contributions started speaking for themselves again.

That conversation could have gone a completely different way – if we had chosen to focus solely on output and not on what was hurting the human behind the numbers.

This experience taught me something essential: People don't always need answers. Sometimes, they just need space. A space that is safe.

A space that doesn't judge. A space where they are more than their performance.

When you approach a difficult conversation with curiosity instead of criticism, the outcome can be transformative.

It's easy to say, "You're underperforming." It takes more effort to say, "I've noticed a change. What's going on? Can I help?"

One is a statement of fault. The other is an invitation to trust.

In people management, your words can either create walls or build bridges. And often, it's not what you say – it's how you choose to show up in the moment that defines whether you're seen as a manager, or remembered as a leader.

Recognition: A Simple Act, a Powerful Result

There is a quiet kind of magic in appreciation – the kind that doesn't make headlines, doesn't cost a penny, and yet has the power to completely transform how someone feels about their work, their worth, and their place in a team.

Yet, so many managers underestimate it.

We often focus on performance metrics, dashboards, escalations, and deadlines – forgetting that behind every project milestone, every line of code, every patient report, every deliverable is a human being: someone who chose to show up, to contribute, to care.

Recognition is not about ego. It's about dignity. It's not about praise for the sake of motivation. It's about saying: "I saw you. You mattered. Your effort did not go unnoticed."

And the impact of this, especially when sincere, is immense.

A few weeks ago, I was having a candid conversation with a peer who made a remark that truly shook me. Referring to younger employees, especially Gen Z professionals, he said rather dismissively, "They don't care about recognition. These days, maybe we need a 'Hall of Shame' to push them to perform." I was stunned. Not because it was radical – but because it was completely misaligned with the spirit of people leadership.

To assume that people don't value appreciation simply because they don't react to traditional formats is to completely miss the point. Every generation values acknowledgment. Every human being – no matter how senior, how junior, how experienced or how new – wants to know they are seen, not just for what they deliver, but for how they deliver it.

At that time, the supervisors of my team had recently initiated a weekly recognition process within my team. We called it the "Quality Wall of Fame." Every week, based on qualitative contributions, certain team members were highlighted. But I did not stop there. I started sending personalized notes to every single one of them.

Not templated messages. But well-thought-out digital notes. These messages were not dramatic. But they were specific. They were personal. And most importantly, they were authentic.

The response? Nothing short of overwhelming.

People began talking about it. Screenshots of the messages were shared among teams. Others forwarded them to their families. A few even told me – with misty eyes – that this was the first time in their careers they had been appreciated directly by a project head.

The ripple effect was undeniable. Performance improved. Initiative increased. Even team morale – which had been shaky post-restructuring – began to steady. There was laughter again in meetings. People began volunteering for stretch assignments. Not because they were told to – but because they felt valued.

And here's what I realized in that process:

Recognition is not about the reward. It's about the relationship. It's not about points or badges or names on a board. It's about making someone feel that their effort was worth it – that someone noticed, someone cared, someone took time to say thank you.

But of course, the recognition must be genuine.

In the nascent days of my career, when the professional world felt like a vast, uncharted ocean, I was a fresher, paddling hard, often feeling like a small boat in a formidable fleet. The days were long, filled with the earnest intensity of youth – a blend of learning curves, late nights fueled by lukewarm coffee, and an almost desperate desire to prove my worth, to make a meaningful contribution. I poured my energy into every task, driven by an internal compass that pointed towards excellence, though often wondering if my efforts registered beyond my immediate team.

Then, one seemingly ordinary afternoon, amidst the usual flurry of activity and the hum of office life, an email notification popped up. The sender's name made my breath catch: Dr. Rashna Cama, the senior leader of our entire organization. My heart was pumping. Dr. Cama was a figure I, like many others, looked up to with immense respect. To receive a direct email from her was, in itself, significant.

With excitement, I clicked it open. It wasn't a company-wide announcement or a generic memo. It was personal. My eyes scanned the lines, and a warmth began to spread through me. Dr. Cama, in her concise yet impactful way, mentioned specific things I had done – projects I had toiled over, initiatives I had passionately driven. She saw the late hours, the meticulous attention to detail, the willingness to go the extra mile.

And then, there was the line, the one that etched itself onto my memory and, quite literally, onto paper: "You have done the entire organization proud, and I would like to thank you for that."

The words seemed to lift off the screen. "The entire organization proud." It wasn't just acknowledgement; it was a profound validation. In that moment, I wasn't just a junior employee; I was a valued member of a collective, someone whose work resonated at the highest level. A wave of emotion washed over me – surprise, gratitude, and an overwhelming sense of pride that almost brought tears to my eyes. It was as if a spotlight had found me, not to expose, but to illuminate.

The urge to preserve this moment, this feeling, was immediate and powerful. I carefully printed that email. That printed sheet wasn't just a record of a message; it became a touchstone, a personal trophy.

To this day, decades later, that piece of paper, now perhaps a little faded, a little creased at the edges from being moved and cherished, remains with me. It's tucked away safely, a silent testament to a pivotal moment. More than just a feel-good memento, that email became a wellspring of motivation. It ignited a renewed fire. It fueled my determination, not just to meet expectations, but to consistently exceed them.

Genuine appreciation matters like anything across all generations. Appreciation loses its power the moment it becomes a tactic. People can see through flattery, through blanket praise, through hollow acknowledgments. But when appreciation comes from the heart – when it's specific, timely, and real – it transforms people.

It becomes a moment of pride.

A source of motivation.

Sometimes even a turning point.

So, no – we don't need a "Hall of Shame." We need spaces of dignity. We need more leaders who pause to say, "Well done," not after an appraisal cycle, but in real time – when the effort is fresh, the emotion is alive, and the connection is honest.

Because sometimes, the difference between someone quitting quietly and someone going the extra mile is just one line of appreciation.

And as people leaders, that line is always ours to give.

Different People, Different Needs

One of the most beautiful and humbling aspects of leadership is realizing this simple truth:

No two people are the same.

Each team member you manage walks into work every day carrying their own story. Some wear their emotions on their sleeves, others bury their worries behind a composed smile. Some seek feedback constantly because they crave validation and growth. Others prefer quiet space, only surfacing when they feel truly ready.

As a manager, your job is not to standardize people. It's to understand them.

I once had two team members who couldn't have been more different – Roshan and Vinitha.

Vinitha thrived on detail. She wanted clarity in goals, timelines, expectations, and milestones. She sent daily updates even when I did not ask for them. And when I missed responding to her summary mail once, she followed up, politely but firmly. For her, structure equaled security. She felt valued when her work was acknowledged, when feedback was regular, and when expectations were unambiguous.

Roshan, on the other hand, was the opposite. He was creative, and thoughtful – but intensely private. He disliked micromanagement. He needed autonomy. If I messaged him too frequently, he would begin to feel stifled. If I did not check in at all, he might start feeling disconnected. Striking the right balance with him started with one decision: to not treat him like Vinitha.

As a leader, you must adapt – not out of obligation, but out of respect for individuality. Uniform communication might feel "fair" on paper, but in practice, it often misses the mark. What motivates one person might overwhelm another. What feels supportive to one may feel intrusive to someone else.

I'm often impressed by Santanu, a young entrepreneur in his mid-twenties who runs a local gymnasium. What makes him so popular is his intuitive ability to deal with each member according to their specific needs. He instinctively knows when to give some members ample liberty and when to apply more pressure for others.

This level of tailored leadership takes effort. It takes observation, intentional one-on-ones, and genuine curiosity about your people's personalities. But when done right, it leads to deeper trust, more meaningful conversations, and a workplace where people feel truly seen.

Because leadership is not about speaking the loudest. It's about tuning in to different frequencies – and making every voice feel heard.

The Silent Messages You Send

We often think of communication as what we say. But some of the most powerful messages we send are through what we don't say.

Your silence. Your expressions. Your availability. Your consistency. These are all part of your leadership language.

For instance, imagine sitting in a one-on-one with your manager, and mid-conversation, they glance at their phone. Then again. And again. They don't say a word – but they don't have to. Their eyes say it all: "Something else is more important than this moment with you."

You did not hear it in words, but the message landed or think about canceled one-on-ones. Maybe you meant to reschedule. Maybe something urgent came up. But when it happens repeatedly, it no longer feels like a scheduling issue – it feels like a priority issue. And the team member, no matter how professional, begins to withdraw.

One of the most overlooked leadership truths is this: Presence communicates more than position. When you're present – really present – in a conversation, people open up. They trust you. They feel safe.

Recently, my father has been going through some serious health condition requiring a complicated surgery. Our Vertical Head and a very senior leader, Dr. Swapnil Babasaheb Khot, personally called me to check his health status. But he didn't stop there. He told me, with genuine warmth, that I could approach him for anything and everything, and even if he couldn't directly help, he would simply be there to listen. Imagine the profound sense of relief and gratitude I felt hearing such incredibly kind words from a senior leader like him. It was a lifeline of support in a turbulent time.

Here I must mention another leader, Dr. Neha Achrekar. I never had the privilege to work under her leadership directly, but we have known each other for a long time. During this tough phase, Dr. Neha not only enquired about my father's health status but offered all sorts of emotional support, which was truly the need of the hour. Her empathy shone through, providing comfort and strength when it was most needed, leaving an indelible mark on my heart.

Such things really create a lot of difference. Your tone, your timing, your expressions – all of them matter. Do you raise your eyebrows when someone shares a mistake? Do you lean in when someone talks about their aspirations? Do you offer a smile when someone takes a risk?

You're always communicating. Even when you're silent. Especially when you're silent.

So be intentional. Don't just manage communication – embody it.

Digital Communication in the Hybrid Age

In today's hybrid work world, communication has taken on a new shape – one that is more digital, more written, and often more fragile.

Without physical presence, intent gets lost, tone gets misread, and misunderstandings become more frequent. A simple "Sure." in a message can sound agreeable or annoyed, depending on who reads it. A delay in response can feel like a lack of care. A long email can feel overwhelming; a short one, dismissive.

As people managers, we can't afford to be casual in how we communicate across screens.

Be clear. Be warm. Be prompt. When you write to your team, remember that they don't have the benefit of seeing your face or hearing your tone – so choose your words with intention.

Use full sentences when something is important. Avoid using sarcasm or ambiguity over text. Don't overdo the exclamation marks, but don't be so formal that your message feels cold. Use emojis or gifs if they fit your team culture – or drop a quick voice note if something feels too personal for chat.

Most importantly, use video when it matters. Turn your camera on during difficult conversations, team celebrations, or new joiner connects. Seeing a human face is an emotional cue – it builds connection. It makes the interaction feel real.

Also, be crystal clear in expectations. Summarize verbal agreements in writing. Avoid relying solely on casual chats for work commitments. Create clarity in how the team shares updates, how often they check in, and when a meeting is needed vs. when a message will suffice.

Remote or hybrid doesn't mean distant – unless we let it become that.

Digital leadership is still human leadership. And the best digital communicators today are those who blend clarity with empathy –

who understand that behind every screen is a person longing to be understood.

Building a Culture of Openness

If there is one leadership trait that quietly shapes every part of a team's culture – from innovation to retention to morale – it's openness.

It begins not with a policy, not with a handbook, but with you – the manager.

Your tone becomes the team's tone. Your attitude towards mistakes becomes their comfort with risk. Your response to feedback becomes their trust in speaking up.

When you, as a leader, are open, honest, and respectful, your team doesn't just mirror that – they expand upon it. They start communicating more freely, collaborating more authentically, and performing not out of fear, but out of alignment.

But when the opposite happens – when ideas are dismissed, when feedback is deflected, or when communication is wrapped in ambiguity – teams shrink. They go quiet. They play it safe. They avoid sharing what matters most.

In his transformative book Hit Refresh, Satya Nadella talks about how his leadership journey at Microsoft demanded a cultural refresh – one that could not be achieved without radical openness. He writes: "Leaders have to be willing to learn and to have empathy. Only then can they have the kind of openness that encourages innovation."

Nadella did not come in with all the answers. But he came with humility. He made it okay for his senior leadership team to say, "We don't know yet." He normalized vulnerability in leadership – and in doing so, unlocked a wave of creativity, accountability, and growth across the organization.

That is what true openness looks like. It's not about oversharing. It's about creating a space where people feel safe to be real – about their ideas, their fears, and their aspirations.

In my own journey, I've seen how powerful this can be.

There was a time when I joined as a Manager for a team that was clearly talented – but hesitant. In early meetings, they were polite, but the energy was low. I sensed that they were playing defensively. They agreed to everything, but shared very little. There were no bold ideas, no pushback, no ownership. I could feel that they were waiting for permission to be themselves.

So, I decided to go first.

In one of our team huddles, I acknowledged a decision I had made the previous week that did not go well. I explained my reasoning, shared what I had learned, and said simply, "Next time, I'll do better."

There was silence at first. And then, something changed.

One by one, team members started speaking more openly. Someone offered an alternative idea. Another shared a roadblock they had been hiding. A third teammate admitted they were overwhelmed. I could then see it – we weren't just a group of professionals anymore. We were becoming a team.

Openness is not a checkbox. It's a climate – and as a manager, you control the weather.

Want more creativity in your team? Encourage curiosity. Celebrate the question, "What if we tried it this way?"

Want accountability? Ask for feedback on your own leadership. Make it okay for someone to say, "I think we could have handled that differently."

Want collaboration? Make it okay to say, "I need help."

Because here's the thing: when you're real, they will be too.

And once openness takes root, everything shifts. Conflicts are resolved faster. Innovation increases. Emotional safety becomes a norm. And people begin to grow – not just as professionals, but as people.

So, ask yourself:

- When was the last time I said, "I don't know" in front of my team?
- When did I last admit a mistake – and own it fully?
- Have I asked my team, "How am I doing as your manager?"

These questions may feel vulnerable. But they are also powerful.

Because in a culture of openness, feedback is not feared. It's welcomed. Ideas are not guarded. They are shared. Mistakes are not punished. They are learned from.

And that is where real leadership begins – not with control, but with courageous communication.

Communicate to Connect, Not to Control

If there's one truth that leaders often forget amidst the deadlines, escalations, and planning decks, it's this: Communication is not just about transferring information – it's about building connection.

Too often in corporate corridors, communication is reduced to directives, updates, or policy explanations. We speak to instruct, to align, to manage. But rarely do we pause and ask, "Did I make the other person feel heard, safe, and seen?"

Because at its best, communication is not managerial – it's transformational.

It doesn't just clarify goals. It fosters trust. It doesn't just relay tasks. It reflects values.

And the most powerful leaders – the ones who are remembered and not just obeyed – are those who speak to connect, not to control.

One of the greatest lessons on communication I've ever come across was from Dale Carnegie, the legendary author of How to Win Friends and Influence People. He wrote: "Become genuinely interested in other people. Listen more than you talk."

It sounds simple. Almost too simple. But that one line is a cornerstone of great leadership.

Genuine interest is rare. Most of us are trained to speak well. Few of us are trained to listen well – and even fewer to listen without judgment, agenda, or the desire to immediately respond.

But when you listen – truly listen – without interrupting, without correcting, without already formulating your next line of advice, something magical happens. People open up. They feel safe. And most importantly, they feel respected.

As a people manager, your words carry weight. Your silences carry meaning. When you choose to speak, speak not to prove your intelligence but to offer your presence. Speak not to command, but to connect.

Early in my leadership journey, I used to prepare heavily for meetings – charts, facts, talking points. I believed clarity was king. But I slowly realized that what moved people wasn't how well I spoke – it was how sincerely I listened. When I asked "What's going on in your mind?" and sat quietly – that is when the real conversations began.

Over time, I changed how I approached team discussions. Instead of opening with tasks, I began with tone. I'd ask, "How are you feeling today?" or "Is there something on your mind?" I'd stay quiet longer. I'd nod more. And most importantly, I'd resist the urge to fill silences.

And what I discovered was profound.

When people feel heard, they take ownership. When they feel safe, they take risks. When they feel connected, they commit not just to the work – but to the team.

The loudest communicators may dominate meetings. But the most effective communicators transform meetings into spaces of empathy, clarity, and momentum. They understand that communication is not about spotlight – it's about shared space.

Carnegie also taught us that being genuinely interested in people is not a strategy – it's a philosophy. You cannot fake it. Your tone will betray your intent. Your body language will reveal your inner stance.

So, if you're a manager or aspiring leader reading this, ask yourself:

- Do I listen more than I talk?
- Do I invite feedback or just tolerate it?
- Do my words build bridges, or build walls?
- Am I interested in my people's stories, or just their deliverables?

Because ultimately, leadership communication is not about volume – it's about value. Not how much you speak, but how your words make people feel.

When you consistently communicate with empathy, presence, and curiosity – your influence doesn't come from authority. It comes from authenticity.

That is the kind of leader people don't just work for. That is the kind of leader they believe in.

"When someone feels heard, they feel safe." – Simon Sinek

CHAPTER 4

Mentoring Without Spotlight

"A good mentor doesn't give you all the answers – they help you ask better questions." – Steven Spielberg

In the cacophony of the modern corporate arena, where visibility is often mistaken for value and personal brands are meticulously curated for public consumption, the profound art of mentorship risks being overshadowed, or worse, commodified. We are inundated with images of structured programs, metrics-driven developmental plans, and the performative declarations of mentor-mentee pairings on professional networks. Checklists are ticked, feedback sessions are scheduled with ritualistic precision, and success stories are packaged for broad organizational applause. Yet, beneath this veneer of formalized guidance, far from the glare of the corporate spotlight, the most authentic and transformative mentorship often flourishes – unannounced, unpretentious, and deeply resonant.

This chapter delves into that quieter, more potent form of guidance: the mentorship that doesn't announce its arrival with a drumroll or depart with a certificate of completion. It's a mentorship woven into the fabric of daily interactions, a silent current that shapes careers and cultivates character without ever needing to claim credit. It thrives not on fanfare but on genuine human connection, offering steadfast support in the hushed corridors of shared experience, long after the official business hours have drawn to a close. It's the quiet strength that underpins true professional and personal growth, an invisible architecture supporting burgeoning talent, often felt before it's seen, and understood long before it's ever formally acknowledged.

The Quiet Strength: Unraveling the Essence of True Mentorship

Imagine mentorship not as a structured edifice, but as an ecosystem. In this ecosystem, growth is not manufactured; it's nurtured. The truest forms of mentorship bloom organically, often in the unassuming interactions that pepper our workdays. They are found in the patient ear that listens without judgment, the gentle nudge towards a less obvious path, the unwavering belief expressed when self-doubt threatens to engulf. This mentorship is not loud; it doesn't clamor for recognition or seek validation through hashtags and public praise. It's a deeply personal, often reciprocal, exchange built on trust and empathy.

It unfolds in the cadence of ordinary conversations – a shared cup of coffee where a difficult decision is quietly unpacked, a moment of candid feedback delivered with kindness after a challenging meeting, or the unspoken solidarity of a colleague who senses your struggle and offers a silent gesture of support. It's the senior leader who, despite a crushing schedule, carves out moments to genuinely inquire about a junior colleague's well-being, not just their work output. It's the peer who champions your idea in a room where your voice might otherwise be lost. This is the soul of mentorship: an act of seeing and nurturing potential, often when the individual themselves is blind to it. It's the quiet, persistent whisper of "you can" in a world that often shouts "you can't."

Beyond the Blueprint: What Authentic Mentorship Truly Embodies

The architecture of genuine mentorship is not constructed from the rigid beams of authority, the predefined pathways of hierarchy, or the cold mechanics of protocol. Its foundations are far more organic, built upon the bedrock of human presence – the profound act of being truly there for another. It's rooted in the art of deep listening, a willingness to understand the unspoken narratives beneath the surface-level conversations. It's about perceiving the individual beyond their role, their anxieties beyond their achievements, and their aspirations beyond their current capabilities.

Consider the team lead who, after an exhausting day, dedicates an extra hour to help a junior team member polish a crucial presentation, not merely correcting slides, but explaining the underlying strategy, sharing anecdotes of their own early fumbles, and instilling a sense of confidence. Picture the seasoned professional who intuitively senses the awkwardness of a newcomer, navigating the unfamiliar currents of a new workplace, and makes a deliberate effort to foster a sense of belonging – a casual invitation to lunch, an introduction to key informal influencers, a word of encouragement that anchors them in a sea of new faces. Or reflect on the colleague who doesn't settle for the perfunctory "How are you doing?" but pauses, makes eye contact, and genuinely waits for, and listens to, the authentic answer, creating a space for vulnerability and truth.

To step into the role of such a mentor, one doesn't require a litany of accolades, a prescribed number of years in service, or a prestigious title appended to their name. What is indispensable is a heart that is attuned to notice the subtle cues of others, a mind capable of reflective empathy, and an intrinsic willingness to walk alongside someone on their unique, often challenging, journey. Mentorship, in its most impactful form, frequently transcends grand pronouncements or elaborate strategic guidance. It often boils down to reminding someone, sometimes with nothing more than a thoughtfully chosen sentence or a quiet gesture, that their contributions are valued, their potential is recognized, and that they possess the innate strength to take the next uncertain step, and the one after that. It's about illuminating the path, not by flooding it with your own light, but by helping them discover their own.

Deconstructing the Myth of Formal Mentorship

Our corporate landscapes, often driven by a desire for measurable outcomes and scalable solutions, tend to romanticize mentorship as a process that must be institutionalized to be effective. We see the proliferation of formal mentoring programs, matching algorithms, and structured development plans. While these initiatives can provide a valuable framework, offering access and opportunity where it might otherwise be absent, they risk diluting the very intimacy and spontaneity that genuine mentorship thrives upon if they become the only recognized form. The danger lies in believing that mentorship can be wholly contained within, or created by, such structures.

Many individuals find themselves waiting, sometimes passively, to be assigned a mentor, believing that their growth is contingent upon a formally designated guide. Others feel ill-equipped to offer guidance unless anointed with the official title of "mentor." But the spirit of mentorship refuses to be confined by a badge or a job description. It doesn't magically materialize because an HR directive mandates its existence. As Cal Newport compellingly argues in So Good They Can't Ignore You, true career capital – the kind that genuinely propels individuals towards mastery and fulfillment – is often accrued quietly, through diligent effort, focused practice, and experiences that fly beneath the radar of organizational fanfare.

In this context, the most profound mentorship is rarely a declared, contractual arrangement. It's absorbed osmotically, through observation, shared experience, and the gradual building of trust. It's felt in the subtle nuances of behavior, in the consistency of support, in the unspoken confidence conveyed by a respected colleague or leader. Some of the most influential mentors may not even be consciously aware of the full extent of their impact; they are simply embodying their authentic selves – demonstrating integrity, consistency, and a profound humanity in their daily interactions. They do not seek the spotlight, for their deepest satisfaction comes from creating the conditions under which others can discover their own brilliance and shine.

Leading Without Loudness

I recall, with vivid clarity from my earliest days in the corporate world, a manager named Tripti Ghosh. She wasn't just a manager; she became the archetype of quiet, impactful leadership in my mind. Tripti wasn't the kind of leader who commanded attention through charismatic speeches or grand, visible gestures. Her influence was far more subtle, yet palpably profound. Soft-spoken, deeply thoughtful, and possessing an almost preternatural ability to observe, her presence in any meeting or discussion carried an intrinsic weight – not because she demanded focus, but because she so generously offered hers.

Tripti was my very first manager, and I was stepping into my first production role, eager and anxious in equal measure. As was standard for new trainees, we were assigned a reduced target, around 30% of the full quota, to allow us to find our footing. Fueled by a potent combination of ambition and a desire to prove my worth, I completed my assigned tasks well before the deadline. I remember the flush of pride as I messaged her, announcing my early completion. Another manager might have offered a simple acknowledgment, perhaps a word of praise. Tripti's response was different. She acknowledged my effort, yes, but then she gave me more work. Not as a punitive measure, nor as a mere means to fill my time, but as an implicit recognition of my capacity, a gentle challenge because she had already discerned something I had yet to fully understand about myself: my drive, and my nascent potential.

She had also, with her keen observational skills, identified my workaholic tendencies from day one. While many managers might overtly or covertly celebrate such relentless dedication, seeing it as a direct route to increased productivity, Tripti possessed a more holistic, more humane perspective. She was attuned to the risk of burnout, the silent erosion of well-being that can accompany unchecked ambition. There were numerous occasions when, lost in the intensity of my work, I would feel a gentle presence behind me. She would silently walk over, place a hand softly on my shoulder, and with a voice laced with genuine concern, say, "Go, boy. Take a break. Give yourself some time."

That small, almost imperceptible gesture – that subtle, unwavering concern for my well-being beyond my output – has resonated with me for years. It was a profound lesson: Tripti wasn't just managing tasks and targets; she was nurturing a human being. She understood that sustainable performance is intrinsically linked to personal well-being.

Years later, when I found myself at a career crossroads, seeking a more senior role, it was Tripti who, without any fanfare, stepped in. She leveraged her network, offered her guidance, and quietly facilitated an introduction that led to a significant opportunity for me. True to her nature, she never broadcasted her role in this transition. She never sought acknowledgment or public gratitude. That was the essence of Tripti. Her acts of support weren't transactional; they were an authentic expression of her character. She helped not to be known for helping, but because it was an integral part of who she was.

The Manager as Mentor

Whether you consciously embrace the title or not, if you're in a position where you manage people, you're, by default, mentoring them. Every interaction, every decision, every piece of feedback – verbal or non-verbal – serves as a lesson. Your words carry weight, your tone sets a precedent, and your reactions to challenges and successes alike are closely observed and absorbed by your team. The pertinent question, therefore, is not whether you're mentoring, but rather, what kind of mentor are you choosing to be, moment by moment?

You're mentoring when you:

- Pause to truly listen, resisting the urge to immediately formulate a reply or solution, thereby validating their perspective and encouraging thoughtful articulation.
- Offer second chances when an individual falters, framing mistakes not as failures but as crucial opportunities for learning and growth.
- Acknowledge and appreciate effort, even when the desired outcome is not immediately achieved, reinforcing resilience and a growth mindset.
- Step back and create space for others to lead, even if their approach is not yet perfectly polished, demonstrating trust and fostering autonomy.
- Share your own vulnerabilities and lessons learned from past mistakes, demystifying leadership and making it more accessible.
- Champion their work and visibility within the broader organization, acting as an advocate for their talents.

Mentorship, viewed through this lens, ceases to be a formal designation or an additional task on an already crowded to-do list. It becomes an intrinsic way of being, a fundamental aspect of authentic leadership. It's the conscious, daily choice to see individuals not merely as resources to be deployed, but as whole human beings, each with a unique constellation of dreams, fears, capabilities, and untapped potential waiting to be unlocked.

The Alchemy of Micro-Moments

Transformative mentorship doesn't always require grand, orchestrated speeches or elaborately planned developmental workshops. More often, its power lies in the accumulation of micro-moments – brief, seemingly incidental interactions that, over time, sculpt understanding and build confidence. A single, well-timed sentence can echo through a career, offering guidance and encouragement long after it was spoken. Consider the impact of phrases like: "I trust you to handle this responsibility." "You navigated that difficult situation with remarkable poise." "You're far more capable than you currently believe."

Mentorship often materializes when we least expect it: a probing question asked during an informal coffee break that sparks a new line of inquiry, a constructive suggestion offered with empathy during a high-stakes project review, or even the patient, supportive silence that allows someone to stumble, self-correct, and ultimately find their own solution. In his seminal work, Deep Work, Cal Newport underscores the profound importance of focused, undistracted attention in producing work of significant value. This principle applies with equal, if not greater, force to the art of mentoring. The most effective mentors are not necessarily those who schedule rigid, monthly check-ins, but those who offer their complete, undivided presence when it truly matters – be it for five minutes or fifty. In these concentrated moments of genuine connection and focused attention, lessons are not just heard; they are absorbed, integrated, and retained.

It's impossible for me not to speak here of Shri Gurudas Chakrabarty, a name synonymous with inspirational HR leadership. During the zenith of his career, while holding the esteemed position of General Manager, HRD, for Bank of Baroda, he remained an accessible and deeply invested mentor to countless individuals, many of whom did not fall within his direct reporting line. His extraordinary ability to give his undivided attention while keenly observing people – their talents, their challenges, their unspoken aspirations – made him a true "people mentor." A striking example of his impact involved a banker working in the personnel department in Kolkata. This individual was, by conventional measures, far from the visible radar of someone at Shri Chakrabarty's elevated position in Mumbai. However, once Shri Chakrabarty observed him, he immediately recognized his intrinsic value and untapped potential. Without delay, he initiated the process to bring this individual into the HRD function in Mumbai. He then personally invested his time and wisdom in grooming him. Within a remarkably short span of fewer than five years, that banker ascended to significant heights in his career – a trajectory directly attributable to Shri Chakrabarty's discerning eye and dedicated mentorship. Yet, true to the spirit of quiet influence, Gurudas never once spoke of his pivotal role in this gentleman's success. This profound humility, this selfless dedication to nurturing talent without seeking accolades, is what firmly establishes him in my memory as one of the most exceptional people leaders I have ever had the privilege to know.

Why Some Managers Avoid the Mentoring Mantle

Despite the inherent nature of their role, many managers hesitate to consciously embrace the mantle of mentorship. A common barrier is the self-imposed prerequisite of flawlessness – the belief that one must have all the answers, a perfect track record, before presuming to guide others. But mentorship is not a lecture from a pedestal of perfection. It's, at its heart, an act of shared humanity, an invitation to vulnerability. It involves generously sharing the wisdom gleaned from your own journey – successes and setbacks alike – and being transparent about the areas where you, too, are still learning and evolving.

Some leaders harbor concerns about overstepping professional boundaries, unsure of how to navigate the delicate balance between guidance and intrusion. Others feel constrained by the relentless pressure of time, believing that mentorship requires extensive, dedicated blocks that their schedules simply cannot accommodate. But time, much like trust, is cultivated through small, consistent deposits. You don't need hours of uninterrupted sessions to mentor effectively. What you need is intention, presence, and an open heart. The simple act of being fully present in a ten-minute conversation can be more impactful than an hour of distracted, superficial interaction.

The liberating truth is that the more authentic and real you're, the more valuable your mentorship becomes. People do not learn from an illusion of your perfection; they learn from the candid narrative of your journey, with all its imperfections, detours, and hard-won insights. Your willingness to share your own struggles can create a safe space for others to acknowledge theirs, fostering a culture of learning and resilience.

Weaving Mentorship into Your Leadership DNA: Practical Starting Points

You don't need to orchestrate a radical transformation of your leadership style to begin mentoring with greater intention. The most profound shifts often begin with small, consistent changes in behavior and perspective. Consider these starting points:

- Elevate Your Conversations: Move beyond purely transactional discussions about deliverables and deadlines. Ask your team members about their broader aspirations: What skills do they want to develop? What kind of impact do they hope to make? What does success look like for them, personally and professionally?
- Invite Wholeness: Create an environment where individuals feel safe to bring their whole selves to work – their passions, their concerns, their unique perspectives. This fosters deeper trust and allows for more meaningful connections.
- Reframe Feedback: Deliver feedback not as criticism, but as an investment in their growth. Focus on specific behaviors and their impact, and collaboratively explore ways to develop and improve. Ensure feedback is timely, actionable, and always delivered with respect and a positive intent.
- Cultivate a Learning Lab: Explicitly create room for experimentation and, inevitably, mistakes. Frame these not as failures to be penalized, but as invaluable data points for learning. Guide your team members through the process of analyzing what

went wrong and how to approach similar challenges differently in the future.

- Master Proactive Listening: Practice listening not just to respond, but to truly understand. This means paying attention to non-verbal cues, asking clarifying questions, and summarizing what you've heard to ensure mutual understanding.

When you consciously embed these practices into your daily interactions, mentorship ceases to be a separate, delineated activity. It becomes an organic, intrinsic component of your leadership DNA, shaping your decisions, your communication, and the very culture of your team.

The Deepest Impact Bears No Signature

Ultimately, the mentors who leave the most indelible marks on our lives are not always remembered for the dazzling brilliance of their technical expertise or the strategic masterstrokes of their careers. They are cherished for something far more fundamental: how they made others feel. They are remembered for instilling a sense of capability in the face of daunting challenges, for offering unwavering encouragement when spirits flagged, and for nurturing a belief in one's own potential, often before that belief had fully taken root.

You do not require a formal program, an official title, or a designated mentee to step into this powerful role. The simple, yet profound, acts of showing up with genuine presence, paying compassionate attention, and quietly believing in someone's inherent worth and capacity for growth can catalyze transformative change. It's in these unseen currents of support and belief that true potential is often awakened and nurtured.

Let me introduce Dr. Rahul Chowdhury here. During my first job as a Clinical Research Coordinator, I met Dr. Rahul, who was working as a senior Sub-Investigator. What began as a professional relationship quickly blossomed into a brotherly bond. For nearly two decades, even after parting ways professionally, our connection has remained steadfast. Now a senior oncologist, Dr. Chowdhury continues to offer guidance and unwavering support—truly like family.

He always saw something in me, often assuring me that I was destined for great heights. It's a testament to the profound impact of a leader who genuinely believes in and cares for his people. His influence bears no official stamp, no dotted-line reporting, no formal review. Yet it shaped my confidence and direction more deeply than many formal roles ever could.

This quiet, unassuming form of leadership – this mentorship without a spotlight – doesn't seek accolades or leave a visible signature on the achievements of others. Its legacy is far more subtle, yet infinitely more profound. It's etched in the confidence of those you've guided, in the resilience of those you've supported through setbacks, and in the quiet ripple effect as they, in turn, pay that wisdom and encouragement forward, nurturing the next generation of talent in their own authentic way. This is the enduring power of mentorship that operates from the heart, leaving a legacy not of personal glory, but of collective empowerment.

"A great mentor helps you to achieve what seems impossible." – *Mariela Dabbah*

Part II

Driving Growth and Motivation

CHAPTER 5

Motivation – Lighting the Fire Within

"People are motivated by fear but they are not inspired by it."
– Lance Secretan

The True Nature of Motivation

Converse with any leader, from the seasoned executive to the newly appointed team supervisor, about their most persistent challenges, and the word "motivation" will invariably echo through the conversation. It's the managerial philosopher's stone: How does one cultivate an environment where a team remains consistently engaged, perpetually inspired, and performing at their zenith? How do you sustain this vibrant energy, especially when tasks become routine, pressures mount relentlessly, and the horizon of rewards seems distant or uncertain?

The answer, while seemingly straightforward, delves into the profound depths of human psychology: motivation is not a commodity to be distributed or a command to be enforced. It's an inherent potential, a latent energy that a leader must learn to skillfully ignite. It's less about pushing a boulder uphill and more about clearing the path for an already eager river to flow.

At its core, human beings are wired for purpose. We thrive when we perceive that our endeavors carry significance, that our individual contributions are integral to a larger whole, and that our efforts, seen and unseen, are genuinely acknowledged. This is not about a transactional relationship built on bartering efforts for rewards or coercing compliance through the threat of repercussions. It's about a profound understanding of the unique constellation of drives within each individual, and then artfully weaving their daily tasks into the tapestry of that inner drive, making work an extension of their aspirations, not a deviation from them.

Intrinsic Yearning vs. Extrinsic Allure

Motivation flows from two primary wellsprings: the internal landscape of intrinsic desire and the external environment of extrinsic incentives.

Intrinsic motivation is the silent hum of the soul's engine. It's the quiet joy of untangling a complex problem, the surge of pride in surmounting a formidable challenge, the deep satisfaction derived from extending a helping hand to a struggling teammate, or the sheer pleasure of learning and growth. When an individual is intrinsically motivated, they become a self-propelled force. Initiative blossoms, creativity flourishes, and commitment deepens, not because of surveillance, but because the work itself resonates with their inner values and passions. They are architects of their own engagement.

Extrinsic motivation, conversely, is animated by the pull of external rewards or the push of potential consequences. These are the tangible and often public markers: salary increments, coveted promotions, prestigious awards, public praise, or, on the flip side, the desire to sidestep criticism or penalties. While extrinsic motivators can undoubtedly provide a short-term surge in activity or compliance, they seldom cultivate the deep-seated passion, unwavering loyalty, or innovative spirit that defines a truly thriving individual or team. They can be like a sugary treat – a quick burst of energy followed by a potential slump if not backed by more substantial nourishment.

The artful manager, therefore, endeavors to primarily tap into the rich reservoir of their team's intrinsic drivers. Extrinsic tools, such as specific recognition for a job well done or bonuses for exceptional team achievements, are then utilized not as the primary fuel, but as powerful reinforcements and affirmations of the intrinsic value already being demonstrated. They are the spotlight that occasionally illuminates the already burning fire, not the match attempting to light damp wood.

Timeless Wisdom on Inspiring Action

The quest to understand and influence human motivation is far from a modern preoccupation. Ancient Indian philosophy, particularly the astute teachings found in Kautilya's Arthashastra, offers four sophisticated and enduring strategies for guiding and inspiring individuals. These are Sama (conciliation and gentle persuasion), Dana (gifting and rewards), Danda (discipline and consequence), and Bheda (creating division or strategic differentiation, often by highlighting comparisons or alternative paths).

In the contemporary management theatre:

- Sama translates to the art of inspiring through clear, empathetic communication. It's about appealing to logic, shared values, and mutual understanding. It involves coaching, mentoring, and fostering a climate where concerns are heard and addressed respectfully. It's the quiet conversation that aligns individual purpose with collective goals.

- Dana manifests as the thoughtful offering of recognition, incentives, and opportunities. This is not just about monetary rewards; it includes developmental assignments, public acknowledgment tailored to individual preferences, or even the gift of increased autonomy. The key is that the "gift" is perceived as valuable and equitable by the recipient.

- Danda represents the principle of establishing clear, fair, and consistently applied consequences for persistent underperformance or detrimental behavior. It's not about ruling by fear, but about upholding standards and ensuring accountability for the collective good. Used judiciously, transparently, and as a last resort, Danda reinforces the importance of shared commitments.

- Bheda, in a constructive modern context, is the nuanced art of showing contrasts or possibilities to illuminate a path forward. This could involve showcasing another team's success as a source of learning and inspiration (not invidious comparison), illustrating the tangible benefits of adopting a new process, or outlining the missed opportunities if a current trajectory remains unchanged. It's about creating a constructive tension that encourages reflection and positive change.

These ancient strategies, when wielded with wisdom, integrity, and a genuine intent to uplift, are not manipulative tactics. They are sophisticated instruments in a leader's toolkit, designed to help individuals see more clearly, feel more deeply, and act in greater alignment with the team's shared mission and their own potential.

The Pillars of Engagement

Contemporary behavioral science, through decades of research, provides robust empirical support for what intuitive and empathetic managers have long understood. Three psychological needs stand out as universal drivers of high performance and sustained motivation: Autonomy, Mastery, and Purpose.

- Autonomy is the innate human desire for self-direction. It's about providing individuals with the latitude to make meaningful choices about their work – how they approach tasks, organize their time, and contribute their unique skills. It means trusting them to own their outcomes. Micromanagement, the antithesis of autonomy, is a relentless corrosive agent that eats away at initiative, creativity, and morale. Cultivating autonomy requires building a foundation of psychological safety where individuals feel empowered to act and even make mistakes without fear of undue reprisal.
- Mastery speaks to our inherent urge to improve, to develop our competencies, and to become demonstrably better at something

that holds meaning for us. People remain deeply engaged when they can witness their own growth, achieve milestones (however small), and feel a sense of progress in their craft. This involves providing challenging yet achievable tasks, opportunities for skill development, constructive feedback, and celebrating the journey of learning.

- Purpose is the profound, often unspoken, "why" that underpins our efforts. It's the feeling that "what I do here, in this role, on this team, in this organization, matters." A task might appear mundane in isolation, but if it demonstrably contributes to a customer's satisfaction, a colleague's success, the organization's mission, or a broader societal good, it becomes imbued with value.

When managers consciously design roles and orchestrate the work environment to connect daily tasks with these three fundamental drivers, something remarkable happens. People aren't pushed by external pressures; they are pulled forward by an intrinsic sense of meaning, competence, and self-determination.

A Symphony of Quiet Motivation

Several years ago, I had the privilege of working with a team member named Alli. He was a bastion of technical brilliance, utterly dependable, yet profoundly quiet. He rarely spoke in meetings, seldom initiated questions, and preferred the company of a small, familiar circle. To some, he might have appeared disengaged, perhaps even indifferent. But I sensed a different current beneath the still surface.

One afternoon, during an informal chat, I gently probed, "Alli, what aspects of your work do you find most engaging, the parts that really absorb you?" After a thoughtful pause, his eyes lit up subtly. "Finding the subtle errors in the most complex transactions, especially those processed by someone else who is generally very accurate. It's like solving an intricate puzzle that no one else has quite cracked." That was the key, the window into his intrinsic world. Recognizing this, I began to channel more analytical, investigative tasks his way, often above and beyond his standard responsibilities, framing them as unique challenges only he could unravel.

Years passed, and Alli eventually moved to another organization. Then, unexpectedly, my phone rang. It was Alli. He had been offered a significant new role, one centered entirely on deep-dive analysis and investigation of critical transactional discrepancies that had led to major issues. He confessed his hesitation, a flicker of self-doubt about stepping into such a high-stakes position. Drawing upon my memory of his unique strengths, I offered my unequivocal reassurance.

As anticipated, Alli did not just perform in his new role; he excelled, earning widespread praise and numerous accolades. Colleagues began to seek out his expertise. Within six months, his confidence blooming, he was proactively proposing systemic improvements to prevent future issues. Today, organizations actively court him; he is now flooded with offers, a testament to his specialized and now visible talent.

Meeting him in person a few weeks ago was a revelation. The quiet, almost invisible individual from years past had transformed into a confident, sought-after expert. Alli was never unmotivated; he was, like so many others, an intricate instrument waiting for a perceptive conductor, a unique talent waiting to be seen and given the right stage upon which to perform.

I frequently encounter individuals who express a sense of demotivation in their current roles. My experience with Alli, and many others since, has taught me that often, they are not truly lacking motivation in its purest sense. Rather, they are yearning for their unique capabilities and passions to be recognized and meaningfully engaged. However, the path to such breakthroughs is a two-way street. When I have offered tailored support or challenging assignments to some, designed to tap into what I perceived as their latent interests, a surprising number have shied away, hesitant to step beyond their comfort zones. Alli never did that. He embraced each new puzzle, each complex challenge, with quiet diligence and in doing so, he carved his path to extraordinary success.

The Manager's Missteps: Unintentional Dampeners on the Flame

In their earnest, often well-intentioned efforts to bolster motivation, managers can inadvertently achieve the opposite, dousing the very sparks they wish to fan.

- One common error is the inflation of praise or the indiscriminate distribution of rewards. When every minor action is lauded with the same effusive enthusiasm, or rewards become predictable entitlements, both lose their significance. Genuine recognition feels diluted, and exceptional contributions go unremarked, fostering cynicism rather than encouragement. Praise should be specific, sincere, and proportionate to the effort or achievement.
- Another prevalent mistake is projecting one's own motivational drivers onto others. A manager who thrives on high-stakes challenges and public recognition might assume their team members share this exact profile. However, another individual might find deeper fulfillment in stability, collaborative harmony, deep technical work, or private, thoughtful acknowledgment. Assuming uniformity is a recipe for mismatched incentives.
- A third critical oversight is ignoring the invisible effort and the silent battles. Many individuals contend with self-doubt, anxiety, personal hardships, or the creeping tendrils of burnout, yet they continue to show up and contribute. If these quiet struggles for resilience and consistency go unacknowledged and unsupported, their inner motivation can gradually erode under the weight of unseen burdens.

- Finally, ambiguity in goal-setting or expectations is a potent demotivator. People need clarity: What precisely is expected of them? Why is this task important in the larger scheme? How will success be defined and measured? Without this clarity, effort can feel directionless and progress intangible, leading to frustration and disengagement.

I recall a manager I supervised some years ago. He genuinely considered himself a "great people manager." Yet, observing him closely revealed a pattern of well-meaning blunders. Each morning, he would make his rounds, showering his team members with a torrent of generic, flowery compliments, regardless of their actual performance or contributions that day. His underlying belief was that a constant stream of praise would keep everyone happy, intrinsically motivated, and performing at their peak, thereby making his own managerial life easier. This approach, predictably, was ineffective. People can distinguish between genuine appreciation and superficial flattery. Moreover, a one-size-fits-all approach to praise ignores the diverse personalities and needs within a team. Authentic connection and tailored acknowledgment are key; blanket flattery rarely resonates deeply.

Unlocking Individual Drive

The only genuinely reliable method to understand what animates an individual is deceptively simple: ask with genuine curiosity, and then listen with profound attention. This is not a cursory check-in; it's an exploration.

Transform your one-on-one meetings from status updates into opportunities for deeper dialogue. Gently explore their aspirations, their passions beyond the current task list. What kind of work truly excites them and makes them lose track of time? Where do they envision their professional growth heading? What specific accomplishments, past or present, have given them the most profound sense of satisfaction and pride?

Recognize that ambition is not monolithic. Not everyone is energized by the prospect of climbing the corporate ladder. Some crave mastery in their chosen craft, seeking depth over breadth. Others thrive on variety and new challenges, relishing the opportunity to learn different skills. Some are driven by the tangible impact their work has on others. Still others prioritize work-life integration and a sense of balance.

When you can thoughtfully align an individual's responsibilities and opportunities with their unique, intrinsic drivers, you unlock a qualitatively different level of energy, creativity, and ownership. Work ceases to be a mere obligation and transforms into a vehicle for personal fulfillment.

If you're privileged to lead a team, your first crucial investment is to understand each member as an individual. Delve, respectfully, into their background – not intrusively, but to understand the context from which they've come. What experiences have shaped them? What brings them genuine joy, both inside and outside of work? This deeper understanding will illuminate the unique levers of motivation for each person. Yes, there will inevitably be times when you discover that certain factors motivating some members are beyond your direct sphere of influence – perhaps compensation structures or broader organizational policies. That is perfectly acceptable. Acknowledge these limitations transparently, and then channel your energy into creatively addressing the many factors that are within your control. Significant improvements can emerge from this focused effort.

During the "Great Resignation" period of 2020-2021, many organizations, ours included, saw valued employees depart for what appeared to be solely more lucrative offers elsewhere. While understandable, what was more concerning was the reaction of some managers who resigned themselves to the situation, lamenting that people were motivated only by money – a factor largely outside their immediate control. This was a reductive and disempowering view. While financial considerations are undeniably a component of the overall motivational equation, they are rarely the sole or even primary driver for sustained engagement. Numerous other aspects – a supportive culture, meaningful work, recognition, flexibility – were very much within their control and could have been leveraged more effectively.

The Power of Micro-Moments: Small Gestures, Monumental Impact

Cultivating motivation doesn't always necessitate grand, elaborate initiatives or sweeping policy changes. Often, its most potent forms are found in the consistent accumulation of seemingly small, thoughtful micro-moments.

A timely and specific "thank you," acknowledging not just the outcome but the effort or insight involved. A public acknowledgment during a team meeting, highlighting how an individual's contribution specifically advanced a shared goal. A manager stepping in to say, "I noticed the extra care you took on that report – it made a significant difference in its clarity." These seemingly minor actions powerfully reaffirm an individual's worth and visibility.

Even the act of entrusting someone with a new responsibility, perhaps leading a small, ad-hoc task force or mentoring a new team member, sends a resonant message: "I see your potential. You're ready for this. I believe in you."

These moments of genuine recognition and trust have a shelf life far exceeding the duration of any single project. They embed themselves in an individual's professional self-image. They are the subtle threads that weave a strong fabric of commitment and psychological safety.

As Carol Dweck so astutely observes in her seminal work, Mindset, "Praise effort, not just innate intelligence or talent, and you'll build drive that lasts." Focusing on the process, the perseverance, and the strategies employed, rather than just the outcome or perceived brilliance, cultivates a growth mindset where challenges are seen as opportunities for development, not tests of fixed ability.

Architecting an Environment Where Motivation Flourishes

Ultimately, motivation cannot be mechanically injected or demanded. It must be organically cultivated. It's an emergent property of a well-tended environment.

As a leader, your paramount role shifts from being a "motivator" to becoming an "architect of motivation." This involves thoughtfully designing and consistently nurturing an ecosystem where people:

- Feel psychologically safe to experiment, to propose unconventional ideas, and yes, even to fail without fear of disproportionate judgment – understanding that mistakes are data points for learning.
- Are appropriately challenged to stretch their abilities and grow, without being pushed to the point of feeling overwhelmed or crushed by unrealistic expectations.
- Are effectively supported with resources, guidance, and mentorship, without being coddled or spoon-fed, thereby fostering independence and problem-solving skills.
- Are sincerely recognized for their contributions and efforts in ways that resonate with them personally, without feeling patronized or subjected to insincere platitudes.

When individuals operate within such an environment – one built on trust, guided by clear purpose, and characterized by genuine appreciation – they naturally bring their most engaged, creative, and energetic selves to their work. And when that occurs, exceptional results invariably follow, not as a forced outcome, but as a natural consequence.

Spark the Innate Flame, Don't Force the Fire

True motivation is not a roaring inferno ignited by decree, fueled by elaborate incentive structures, or maintained under the cold pressure of fear. Such forced fires often burn brightly but briefly, leaving behind only ash and resentment. The art of fostering enduring motivation resides in a quieter, more profound understanding of what truly stirs the human spirit. It's found in the deliberate, empathetic acts of connecting with people at a fundamental level, recognizing their unique drivers, and creating pathways for their daily work to intersect with their deeper sense of purpose, passion, and potential. This approach is built on an unwavering belief in the capacity of individuals, a conviction that, as Robert Iger aptly describes in The Ride of a Lifetime, acts as a "force multiplier," infusing a team with positive energy, resilience, and a shared sense of possibility.

I witnessed this firsthand in a previous manager, Basharat Andrabi, who now holds a senior leadership position in a highly reputed multinational corporation. Basharat possessed an almost alchemical ability to inspire – he could, metaphorically speaking, motivate a piece of stone. More than a decade ago, during a period when the atmosphere on our project was becoming undeniably toxic, he was our crucial agent of detoxification. It was not through lengthy pronouncements or imposed team-building exercises. Instead, he would have several brief, genuine chats with each of us throughout the day. You would walk away from these interactions feeling an undeniable surge of motivation, a renewed sense of purpose and capability.

This was not a strategy effective only for his direct reports or more junior colleagues. Even recently, navigating a period of career uncertainty, I sought his counsel. An hour-long meeting in Mumbai was enough. In that relatively short time, he did not offer a magic formula or a prescriptive path. He simply, through his presence and insights, made me understand my own inherent value and potential once again, effectively reigniting the fire that had been flickering within me. It's a rare and invaluable pleasure to encounter such leaders – those who possess the wisdom and empathy to connect with each individual uniquely and unlock their personal source of drive.

As a leader, your most critical responsibility is not to implement a single, universal motivational program. It's to become a student of your people – to learn the unique rhythm of their aspirations, to understand the diverse tapestry of their dreams, and to uncover the individual "why" that gives their work meaning. Armed with this insight and guided by genuine empathy, you must then dedicate yourself to finding or creating the bridges that allow them to connect their heart to their work, their personal spark to the collective endeavor. This is how you build a truly motivated and thriving team – by nurturing the flames that already exist, rather than attempting to impose a fire from the outside.

> *"It's the job of the manager not to light the fire of motivation, but to create an environment to let each person's personal spark of motivation blaze." – Frederick Herzberg*

CHAPTER 6

Delegation – Trust, Ownership, Growth

"If you want to go fast, go alone. If you want to go far, go together."
– African Proverb

This ancient wisdom, echoing through generations, holds a profound truth for anyone in a position of leadership. The journey of a team, a department, or an entire organization is not a sprint accomplished by a solitary star, but a marathon powered by collective strength. And at the heart of this collective strength lies a practice often misunderstood, yet utterly transformative: delegation.

The Misunderstanding Around Delegation

In the bustling corridors of modern workplaces, delegation frequently wears a disguise. For some, it's mistaken for a clever sleight of hand, a way for managers to shed burdensome tasks, appearing as thinly veiled laziness or an outright avoidance of responsibility. Many first-time managers, eager to prove their worth and fearful of perception, clutch their tasks tightly, worrying that letting go will brand them as merely "pushing work onto others." On the other extreme, some view delegation as a golden ticket to a clear desk, a mechanism to free up their own time without a thread of continued accountability for the outcome. Both perspectives, however, are flawed, like looking at a magnificent tree and seeing only the fallen leaves, not the deep roots or the sprawling branches reaching for the sun.

Delegation, in its most authentic and potent form, is far removed from these shadowy interpretations. It's a cornerstone leadership skill, a vibrant testament to your belief in the potential of others. It's the quiet language of trust, an articulate expression of your ability to nurture and develop talent, and a bold declaration of your confidence to relinquish exacting control. True delegation is not about offloading work; it's about deliberately investing in people, planting seeds of capability that will one day blossom into a forest of expertise. It's the art of empowering, not a strategy for escape.

Why Managers Hesitate to Delegate

Despite its clear benefits, many managers find themselves trapped within self-imposed barriers, hesitating at the threshold of effective delegation. These are not external constraints, but internal narratives that whisper doubt and caution.

One of the most formidable of these is perfectionism. The silent, often unconscious, belief that "no one can do it as well as I can" becomes a heavy chain, tethering a manager to tasks that could be opportunities for others. This manager often finds themselves redoing work, or spending more time correcting minor flaws than it would have taken to coach effectively upfront. Imagine a skilled artisan, so convinced of their unique touch that they refuse to teach their apprentices, ensuring their craft, while impeccable, never scales beyond their own two hands.

Then there is the chilling fear of failure. "If someone on my team makes a mistake, it's my reputation on the line. It reflects poorly on me as their leader." This fear, while understandable, often leads to a suffocating level of oversight or, worse, a complete unwillingness to entrust significant tasks. It prioritizes short-term risk avoidance over long-term team development, forgetting that a ship is safe in the harbor, but that is not what ships are built for.

Some managers grapple with an emotional attachment to responsibilities that once defined their individual success. These tasks were their stepping stones, the arenas where they shone. Letting go can feel like losing a part of their identity, a tangible connection to their past achievements. They might think, "This is my specialty; this is what got me here." But leadership asks us to evolve, to find new ways to contribute, not by clinging to old glories but by cultivating new ones in others.

Of course, there is the deceptively pragmatic thought: "It's quicker to do it myself." In the immediate, frantic rush of a deadline, explaining a task, outlining expectations, and being available for questions can seem like an inefficient detour. "I can knock this out in an hour," the manager thinks, "but it'll take two hours to explain it and then review it." This short-term calculation often ignores the compound interest of time saved in the future when a team member is fully capable.

These internal monologues, these seemingly rational justifications, may offer fleeting comfort or a brief illusion of control. But in the long run, they cultivate a landscape of dependency, stunt the growth of promising individuals, and inevitably lead to a manager who is overwhelmed, overworked, and a bottleneck to progress.

Let me paint a clearer picture with the story of Roohi (let us call her by that name here), a manager who reported directly to me. Roohi was a phenomenon in her role as a first-line manager. Her team operated like a well-oiled machine; every member was synchronized, deliverables were met with flawless precision, and morale was high. Recognizing her incredible capabilities, we promoted her to a role supervising other first-line managers. But this new altitude revealed unexpected turbulence. Roohi, the paragon of efficiency, struggled. She was visibly uncomfortable guiding her new team of managers, often finding herself in tense disagreements. Her perfectionism, once a hallmark of her individual success, became her Achilles' heel. She would dive into the details of their responsibilities, agitated by the slightest deviation from her exacting standards. Ultimately, she would often just take over the work herself, convinced she was setting an example of excellence. She genuinely believed her direct involvement would inspire them. The reality? Her direct reports, experienced managers themselves, felt disempowered, micromanaged, and increasingly disconnected. Their ownership dwindled because their manager was, in essence, doing their jobs. How long could this model sustain itself? Roohi could climb so high on her own efforts, but at what point would the sheer volume of work become impossible for one person, however brilliant, to oversee with such granular control? This is the critical question that individuals who shy away from true delegation must confront.

Delegation as a Compass for Growth, Not an Escape Hatch

When embraced with courage and executed with wisdom, delegation transforms from a managerial chore into a powerful engine for development. It becomes the primary tool to cultivate leadership capacity deep within the team. It's how you build not just skills, but genuine capability – the ability to think critically, solve problems, and take initiative. It creates vital redundancy in critical tasks, ensuring that the team's work is not dependent on a single individual. More strategically, it frees the manager to rise above the immediate fray, to engage in the higher-level thinking, planning, and visioning that their role truly demands.

Think of the unspoken message that genuine delegation sends. It's a clear signal: "I trust you. I see your potential. I believe you can navigate this, and I am here to support your journey." This is not just a morale booster; it's a profound affirmation of worth that fuels confidence and ignites commitment. And when mistakes happen, as they invariably will, they cease to be indictments and instead become invaluable learning opportunities. With constructive feedback loops, these moments of imperfection become crucibles for growth – for the team member who learns resilience and refinement, and for the manager who learns how to better guide, coach, and support.

However, the art of delegation must be wielded with integrity, lest it projects the image of an escapist, someone eager to offload responsibility without true engagement. I recall another manager, let's call him Rohan. Rohan was quick to delegate, often before he had fully grasped the nuances of the work himself. He exuded trust and faith in his team, which was commendable. But a pattern emerged. During crises, when swift, informed decisions were paramount, his team members and even senior stakeholders would bypass him. They knew Rohan would first need to consult his subordinates to understand the situation before offering any input. He became a relay station rather than a strategic leader. He once confessed to me, a touch of sadness in his voice, how it stung when people went around him during emergencies. He felt sidelined, a mere figurehead. The hard truth, which he eventually came to realize, was that he had only himself to blame. Had he understood that delegation required initial understanding and continued strategic oversight, not just handing over, he could have avoided this erosion of his influence. True delegation involves entrusting, not abandoning.

The Blueprint for Effective Delegation: More Than a To-Do List

To delegate with impact requires more than simply handing over a task. It's a thoughtful process, a craft to be honed.

- Clarity is King: The journey begins with absolute clarity. Be crystal clear and remarkably specific about what needs to be done. But don't stop there. Explain why this task matters. What is its significance? What is the desired outcome? Is it a detailed report, a functioning prototype, a satisfied client? When individuals understand not just the mechanics of the task but its deeper purpose, their investment skyrockets. For instance, instead of saying "Prepare the deliverables report," try: "Please prepare the monthly deliverables report, analyzing trends by quality and productivity, so we can identify our top performers and areas for strategic improvement for next month's plan. The goal is to have actionable insights for our planning meeting next Tuesday."

- Paint the Bigger Picture (Context): People thrive when they see how their individual cog fits into the larger machine. Explain the context. How does this specific task contribute to the team's goals, the department's objectives, or the company's mission? This fosters a profound sense of ownership. They aren't just completing a task; they are contributing to a meaningful endeavor.

- Match Task to Talent (Capability and Potential): Capability is the next crucial filter. Delegating a complex strategic analysis to someone who has only ever handled data entry is setting them up for failure, and you for disappointment. This doesn't mean you only delegate to the most seasoned expert. It means you realistically assess the person's current skills and their potential for growth. Is this a stretch assignment that, with support, they can rise to? Ensure resources, training, or mentorship are available if needed. Sometimes, the greatest growth happens just outside the comfort zone, with a sturdy safety net below.

- The Art of Follow-Up (Without Suffocating): Follow-ups are essential to stay informed, offer support, and ensure things are on track. However, this must not devolve into micromanagement, which breeds resentment and crushes autonomy. Agree on specific check-in points or milestones. These could be brief daily syncs for a critical short-term task, or weekly updates for a longer project. The aim is to be a supportive guide, available to remove roadblocks, not a constant overseer. This also ensures that during any unexpected crisis, you possess updated details, ready to contribute or steer as needed. Ask open-ended questions: "How is it progressing?" "What challenges are you encountering?" "What support do you need from me?"

- Acknowledge, Appreciate, Amplify (Recognition): This is non-negotiable. Delegation without recognition is a recipe for resentment and disengagement. Delegation with sincere appreciation builds loyalty, trust, and a positive cycle of performance. There are countless instances where a manager delegates a significant portion of their own activities, leans heavily on a deputy, yet when the accolades arrive, they stand alone in the spotlight. This is not just poor form; it's a failure of leadership. Giving due credit, publicly and privately, and genuinely appreciating someone's contribution is not a discretionary choice but a fundamental mandate for every manager.

I have been fortunate to witness truly inspiring leaders who instinctively put their people front and center, ensuring their team members – the ones who truly navigated the complexities of the assigned job – receive their well-deserved share of credit. Here, I must once again speak of Ramanarayana Parhi. Mr. Parhi entrusted me with a task so critical and challenging it felt like scaling a sheer cliff face – almost a mission impossible. Yet, his faith during the delegation was palpable, and his instructions on the expectations were always a model of clarity. He checked in, offered guidance, but never hovered. When, against the odds, the task culminated in a resounding positive outcome, Ram did not just send a thank you. He composed a detailed email to all key stakeholders, explicitly highlighting my name and contributions as pivotal to the success. That single gesture, that public acknowledgement, acted like a powerful elixir. It boosted my confidence immeasurably, and more importantly, it inspired me to pass on that same recognition to my own team members who had supported me, creating a beautiful ripple effect of appreciation and motivation.

The Gradual Spectrum of Delegation

Delegation is not a simple on-off switch; it's a dynamic spectrum, a journey that evolves with the maturity and capability of your team.

Level 1: Directive Delegation (High Guidance): Early on, or with less experienced team members, you might assign specific, well-defined tasks with detailed instructions and frequent check-ins. "Please research these three competitors and summarize their key marketing strategies in a one-page document by tomorrow."

Level 2: Guided Delegation (Shared Exploration): As trust and skills grow, you delegate broader objectives, allowing team members more freedom in determining the 'how'. "We need to improve our customer onboarding process. Can you explore some options and present your top three recommendations with pros and cons next week?"

Level 3: Stewardship Delegation (Outcome Focused): Here, you entrust significant responsibilities, focusing on the desired outcomes and granting considerable autonomy in approach and execution. "You're now responsible for overseeing the entire customer onboarding experience. Your goal is to increase customer satisfaction scores by 15% within six months. Keep me updated on your strategy and progress."

Level 4: Empowerment (Proactive Ownership): This is the zenith of delegation. Your team members understand the strategic goals so well, and feel so trusted and empowered, that they proactively identify challenges and opportunities, coming to you with proposed solutions, often before you've even formally asked.

This progression from directive, task-based delegation to strategic, outcome-based empowerment is the hallmark of a healthy, high-functioning team, led by a manager who understands the profound art of letting go to lift others up.

My Personal Encounters with Empowering Delegation

The lessons of delegation are often best learned not from textbooks, but from personal experience, from those leaders who saw something in us we might not have seen in ourselves.

My journey into understanding true empowerment began under Dr. Prasad Apsangikar, a distinguished Head of Medical Affairs at Reliance Life Sciences. I was hardly twenty-something then, new to the corporate world, and admittedly intimidated by the wealth of experience around me. I remember the sheer weight of our first meeting, a moment that would redefine my early career trajectory. Dr. Prasad looked at me, perhaps seeing a potential I hadn't yet recognized in myself, and his first words cut through my apprehension: "Avisek, just don't wait for any instructions. Get into the depth. And when I say depth, I mean it. Don't worry about any seniority or designation. You just get the work done and let me know wherever you need my support." It was more than just a directive; it was a charter of freedom and responsibility. In an environment where a young professional might expect to be micromanaged or given only piecemeal tasks, Dr. Prasad was essentially telling me to take the reins on significant initiatives. The impact was immediate and immense, a surge of confidence that I still struggle to fully articulate. His message was exceptional because it wasn't just about delegating an important function; it was a powerful affirmation of his trust in my nascent abilities, a clear signal that he believed I could deliver.

That foundational trust proved invaluable as my career evolved, and other leaders continued to nurture my growth by pushing me beyond different comfort zones. For instance, I vividly recall working with a manager many years ago, a wonderful human being who sadly is no more with us. His name was Late Chayan Pant. Chayan, with his characteristic insight, once told me during a review, "You're brilliant at execution, truly meticulous, but you seem to shy away in leadership settings, in making your voice heard." I knew he was right. I was often hesitant to take the lead in meetings, preferring to contribute from the sidelines and deferring to more vocal colleagues. During a particularly high-stakes project, Chayan assigned me the lead role in handling a crucial client presentation. A wave of terror washed over me – my palms grew sweaty, my heart pounded. Chayan, sensing my apprehension, could have easily stepped in and taken over, ensuring a "safe" outcome. But he did not. Instead, he offered his time to help me rehearse, not by dictating the content, but by asking probing questions, encouraging me to frame the narrative in my own voice, to own the story. He helped me anticipate questions, refine my key messages, and build my confidence layer by layer. The result? I delivered that client presentation not just competently, but with a newfound confidence that surprised even myself. It was, by all accounts, fantastic. The client was engaged, my points landed, and the internal victory was immense.

A similar defining moment occurred a few months prior. Despite having almost 2 decades of experience, I found myself as the most junior participant in a high-voltage client meeting, surrounded by very senior leadership from both our organization and the client's. Abhishek Garg, who has been not just one of my most brilliant managers but also a cherished mentor, called me just an hour before the meeting and simply said, "You're going to kick this off and present the slides." My mind raced. All he added, was an informal, "You start it off without thinking twice. If there is anything, I am always here to pitch in." Wow. Those few words were like a shot of adrenaline and a warm blanket all at once. The fear did not vanish, but the reassurance that he had my back gave me the courage to step forward. The presentation went smoothly. The client not only appreciated the clarity of the information but also my delivery. Afterwards, several very senior leaders from my own organization took the time to personally congratulate me. All it took was someone else's trust and a gentle, supportive push beyond my perceived limits.

These experiences are not just fond memories; they are permanent lessons etched into my leadership philosophy. I consciously strive to replicate these acts of faith with my own team, knowing that this journey of empowerment is a continuous cycle, passed from one leader to the next.

Delegation as a Strategic Investment

At first glance, especially to the uninitiated or the overly cautious, delegation can indeed seem inefficient. You invest time explaining tasks, clarifying ambiguities, reviewing drafts, coaching team members through hurdles, and sometimes, correcting mistakes. It feels like you could have done it faster yourself. And in that isolated moment, you might be right.

But this perspective is shortsighted. This upfront investment of time and energy is precisely that – an investment. Like nurturing a sapling, it requires patience and care, but the eventual rewards are immense. As individuals grow in competence and confidence under your guidance, they require progressively less supervision. They begin to anticipate needs, to solve problems independently. They start taking initiative, owning their work with a passion that can only come from genuine empowerment. They surprise you with innovative solutions and insightful perspectives you might never have considered.

Eventually, you cultivate something truly remarkable: a team that can not only function effectively but flourish, even thrive, without your constant, hands-on direction. This is not just effective leadership; it's the foundation of sustainable, resilient leadership. It's the difference between being a firefighter, constantly battling blazes, and being an architect, designing a fire-resistant structure.

Cultivating Leaders from Within: The Power of Interim Roles

Early in my career, I observed a leadership strategy that profoundly influenced my approach to team development. I saw senior leaders entrust promising associates with significant leadership responsibilities, even without formal titles or promotions. This wasn't about giving a fancy designation; it was about providing a real-world audition for the next level. It allowed us to truly assess an individual's readiness, their ability to navigate challenges, motivate teams, and ultimately, perform in a leadership capacity, all before committing to a permanent title. This approach eliminated the risk of a new title influencing perceptions, allowing pure performance to shine through.

When I took over a new project in 2019, I noticed a stark contrast. The prevailing culture was to recruit senior talent externally, overlooking the immense potential within our own ranks. This felt like a missed opportunity – a disservice to our dedicated associates and a bypass of organic growth. Drawing on my past observations, I immediately began to shift this paradigm.

I started identifying individuals who exhibited exceptional potential, offering them interim Team Lead or interim Team Manager roles. These weren't symbolic gestures; they came with genuine responsibilities and expectations. My goal was to provide a safe yet challenging environment for them to stretch their abilities. The results were consistently rewarding: most of these associates rose to the occasion, exceeding expectations and demonstrating remarkable growth.

I carried this philosophy into every subsequent project I led, creating a continuous pipeline of internal talent. The most gratifying outcome was watching these individuals not only achieve significant career milestones but also adopt this very practice themselves, nurturing the next generation of leaders within their own teams. This commitment to internal development became a self-sustaining cycle, a flowing river of leadership, proving that investing in your own people isn't just good for the individual; it's transformative for the entire organization.

Creating a Culture of Delegation

For delegation to truly transform an organization, it cannot remain a solo habit practiced by a few enlightened managers. It must be woven into the very fabric of the team's culture.

How do you cultivate such an environment?

- Lead by Example: As a manager, consistently and visibly delegate meaningful work. Talk openly about why you're delegating a particular task to a specific person, highlighting the growth opportunity.
- Encourage Peer-to-Peer Delegation & Mentoring: Foster an environment where team members feel comfortable delegating relevant sub-tasks to their peers, appropriate to their scope. Promote peer mentoring, where those with specific expertise can guide others. This builds collective capability and strengthens team bonds.
- Make it Safe to Ask for Help and to Stumble: Actively create a climate where asking for help is seen not as a sign of weakness, but as a mark of self-awareness and a commitment to quality. Similarly, when a delegated task doesn't go perfectly, frame it as a learning opportunity, not a punishable offense. Conduct blameless post-mortems focused on "what can we learn?" rather than "who is at fault?"
- Recognize and Reward Effective Delegation: When you see a team member successfully take on a delegated responsibility, acknowledge their effort and growth. When you see another team member effectively delegate and empower someone else, praise that leadership behavior.
- Shared Responsibility, Shared Success: Emphasize that responsibility can be shared, and so can success. This fosters a sense of safety and mutual trust – the absolute bedrock of any high-performing team. When individuals know they aren't isolated in their efforts and that the team has their back, they are more willing to stretch themselves and support others.

A culture of healthy delegation builds incredible resilience. It means the team is not crippled by the absence of one person. Knowledge is distributed, skills are multiplied, and the capacity to handle challenges grows exponentially.

A Gentle Nudge for the Overachieving Manager

If you're the person who secretly (or openly) takes pride in being the go-to expert, the one who always has the answer, the indispensable linchpin who works late to ensure everything is perfect – this chapter is especially for you. Your dedication and skill are commendable, but your role as a leader, calls for a different kind of heroism.

Your ultimate effectiveness as a leader is not measured by the sheer volume of what you accomplish, or how many fires you personally extinguish. It's measured by how much you enable others to accomplish, how effectively you build their capacity to solve problems and achieve greatness.

It's okay to step back from the spotlight. It's okay to let others grapple with challenges and discover their own solutions. It's okay for them to make mistakes, as long as they are learning mistakes. It's more than okay – it's essential – to let others shine. Your role is to provide the stage, the lighting, and the supportive applause. It's okay to let go of the need to be the hero of every story.

Leadership is not about making yourself indispensable. True, lasting leadership is about creating an ecosystem, a thriving environment where others can succeed, develop, and lead – even, and perhaps especially, in your absence. That is the profound and enduring legacy of a great manager. As Ravi Venkatesan so aptly puts it in his book, "What the Heck do I do with my Life?": "Empowering others builds your own capacity." It doesn't diminish you; it expands your impact exponentially.

Delegate with Intention, Recognize with Sincerity

Delegation, when approached with thoughtful intention and executed with genuine care, is a powerful force that strengthens not only the individual team members but also the manager and the entire team. It ceases to be a transaction about control and transforms into a partnership centered on shared contribution towards a common, inspiring purpose. It's about crafting a symphony where every instrument plays its part beautifully, contributing to a harmonious whole.

So, the next time you find yourself staring at an overflowing to-do list, feeling the familiar creep of overwhelm, pause. Take a breath. And ask yourself these questions with an open heart:

- Who on my team possesses the raw talent, the nascent skill, that this task could help polish into brilliance?
- Who needs not just a task, but an opportunity, a gentle but firm push to stretch beyond their current horizon and discover new strengths?
- Whose potential is waiting to be unlocked if I simply step aside and create the space for them to rise?
- What unique perspective could someone else bring to this, if given the chance?

And then, having asked, take the leap. Trust them to try. Trust them to learn. Trust them to surprise you.

"No person will make a great business who wants to do it all himself or get all the credit." – Andrew Carnegie

CHAPTER 7

Handling Attrition and Building Loyalty

"People don't quit jobs, they quit managers." – Marcus Buckingham and Curt Coffman

This oft-repeated adage is not just a catchy phrase; it's a profound truth that cuts to the core of organizational dynamics. While strategies, spreadsheets, and systems form the skeleton of a business, it's the human connections, particularly the one between an employee and their direct leader, that provide its lifeblood. When that connection falters, so too does the desire to stay.

Attrition Is Not Just About Numbers

In the sterile environment of a boardroom or during a quarterly review, attrition often gets reduced to a cold, hard metric – a percentage point on a slide, a RAG status on a dashboard. We discuss mitigation strategies and recruitment pipelines, but rarely do we pause to acknowledge the human stories unraveling behind those numbers. Each departure is not merely a statistic; it's a narrative of unmet needs, a severed professional relationship, and a palpable disruption to the intricate ecosystem of a team. The departure of a team member sends ripples far beyond project timelines. It can subtly erode morale, fracture the carefully built cohesion of a team, and introduce an undercurrent of instability that unsettles the entire group.

High attrition is not invariably a symptom of a rival company waving a fatter paycheck. More frequently, it's a distress signal, an alarm bell indicating a deeper, systemic issue. It often whispers of an absence of genuine connection, a fog of unclear expectations, or a pervasive lack of demonstrable care from leadership. It's the slow leak in the ship, often ignored until the water is ankle-deep.

A few years back, I embarked on an Early Warning Signals (EWS) exercise for a critical project. The goal was straightforward: ask supervisors to evaluate their team members – a simple Red, Amber, Green status – to gauge who might be actively exploring other employment avenues versus who felt rooted and stable. The results that came back weren't just surprising; they were a jolt. A staggering 57% of the team members were flagged as 'Red,' indicating they were actively scanning job boards and engaging with recruiters. This included individuals consistently lauded as high-performers, the very people we assumed were content. This wasn't just a number; it was a revelation. It was the sheer magnitude of discontent, and the reasons underpinning it, that truly shook me. This period, notably, wasn't during the peak of the "Great Resignation"; the job market wasn't exactly overflowing with irresistible offers. So, what was fueling this exodus?

Against the well-intentioned advice of my own manager, who believed this task fell squarely within the remit of the supervisors or their direct managers reporting to me, I felt an undeniable pull to connect personally. I sensed the urgency, the need for unfiltered, firsthand insights – a deviation, perhaps, from the principles of delegation I'd previously championed, but a necessary one. These one-on-one conversations were incredibly illuminating. Some concerns were undeniably genuine – career stagnation, a desire for new challenges, or feeling systematically undervalued. Some were understandable, born from personal circumstances or specific project frustrations. And yes, a few were less substantial, perhaps deflection from individuals not meeting performance expectations. For the genuine concerns, I committed to exploring tangible solutions. For those offering fewer convincing reasons, I aimed to provide a broader perspective, helping them see beyond their immediate frustrations.

Following these individual dialogues, I convened a meeting with all supervisors and managers within my team. The objective was clear: to consciously remodel our team culture, fostering an environment of genuine openness and to urgently re-establish and strengthen the bonds between managers and their team members. The outcome? That year, our attrition rate was less than 14%, a stark contrast to the prevailing industry standard of 25%. But more telling than the reduced percentage was the palpable shift in employee satisfaction, the renewed energy, and the collaborative spirit that began to flourish. The numbers told a part of the story, but the improved morale painted the full picture.

Unpacking the Hidden Costs of Attrition

Every time an employee hands in their resignation, it triggers a cascade of consequences, many of which are not immediately apparent.

- Operationally: Delivery schedules are disrupted, project momentum can stall, and crucial skill or knowledge gaps emerge. The remaining team members often shoulder extra work, leading to potential burnout and resentment. The tacit knowledge, the undocumented "how things get done around here," walks out the door with the departing employee.
- Financially: The costs are far more extensive than just a final paycheck. There is the expense of advertising the role, agency fees if used, the significant investment of managerial and HR time in sifting through applications, conducting interviews, and the subsequent onboarding and training for the new hire. Crucially, there is the period of reduced productivity as the new team member gets up to speed – a learning curve that can stretch for months. Some studies suggest the cost of replacing an employee can be anywhere from 50% to 200% of their annual salary.
- Culturally: A departure, especially of a well-liked or influential team member, can significantly weaken team spirit. It can

> breed insecurity among remaining staff ("Are we next? Is there something wrong with this place?"), fuel the rumor mill, and create an atmosphere of "survivor syndrome."

- Emotionally: For the manager, a resignation can feel like a personal blow, triggering self-doubt about their leadership capabilities. For the team, it can erode trust, not just in leadership but sometimes in each other, as they wonder who might be next to leave.

While Human Resources typically manages the administrative process of an exit, it's the direct manager who is left to navigate the emotional turbulence and practical fallout within the team.

Understanding the Real Reasons for Departure

Exit interviews, in theory, are a goldmine of information. In practice, they often yield surface-level, "safe" reasons for leaving: "a better opportunity," "career change," or "relocation." But when you create a space for genuine candor and listen with intent, the underlying currents become visible. People often leave because they don't feel their contributions are seen or valued. Others depart because months have rolled by without a single new skill learned or a challenging project undertaken. Some feel like ghosts in the machine, invisible and unheard, while their colleagues in another corner might be buckling under the weight of excessive workloads and a persistent lack of recognition.

Most departures are not impulsive decisions made overnight. They are usually the culmination of a slow, often painful, emotional uncoupling – a gradual accumulation of disappointments, a slow slide into disengagement, and ultimately, a sense of detachment from the team and the organization's mission.

What continues to astound me is how frequently exit interviews fail to catalyze any concrete, forward-looking action plans. They don't always translate into learnings that could benefit the project, the business unit, a vertical, or even the entire organization. I vividly recall leaving an organization over a decade ago. During my exit interview, I was never truly probed for the actual reasons behind my decision. Yes, I had secured another offer and was leaning towards moving, but no one took the time to delve into the undercurrents of my experience. For over six months, I had been grappling with significant issues within that organization, issues I had escalated to multiple leaders. Each time, I received assurances that they were "looking into it" or "working on it." When I finally tendered my resignation, the official narrative became simply: "leaving for a better offer." The deeper, systemic issues that pushed me towards seeking that offer remained unaddressed.

Exit interviews are too often treated as a bureaucratic checkbox exercise, a formality before an employee walks out the door. In reality, they are invaluable mirrors, reflecting the organizational culture, leadership effectiveness, and employee experience – if leadership is courageous enough to look honestly into that reflection. It's about cultivating an environment where departing employees feel safe enough to be candid without fearing repercussions or burning bridges. Ask them not just why they are leaving, but what made them stay as long as they did. What were the moments of pride? What were the turning points? Look for patterns, for recurring themes in the feedback. If multiple departing employees cite similar experiences with a particular leadership behavior, a specific team dynamic, or a systemic process, that is not a coincidence; it's a call to action.

It's high time, if not already standard practice, for exit interviews across all industries and organizations to be meticulously designed with profound thought and strategic intent. I have no doubt that every organization possesses the right intent; it's the consistent, empathetic, and actionable execution that often requires refinement. Perhaps they should be conducted by a neutral third party, or at least by someone trained in active listening and eliciting honest feedback, with clear pathways for escalating systemic issues.

Steering Towards Reduced Attrition

While managers might not have direct control over salary bands or overarching promotion policies, they exercise immense influence over the daily lived experience of their team members. This daily experience is the fertile ground where loyalty either takes root or withers. You can significantly reduce preventable attrition by consistently practicing a few fundamental, yet powerful, behaviors:

- Cultivate Deep Listening: This goes beyond perfunctory project updates. It means tuning into the unspoken – the emotions, the underlying concerns, the quiet aspirations. Schedule regular, dedicated check-ins that are explicitly about the person, not just the project plan. Ask open-ended questions: "What's energizing you about your work right now?" "What's proving to be a roadblock or a source of frustration?" "What's one thing we could change to make your experience better?" Make genuine time to discuss their career trajectory, their learning preferences, and what truly motivates them. And remember, it's not only permissible but essential to step outside purely professional discourse. Authentic personal connection, sharing a laugh, or acknowledging life outside of work, builds trust and rapport.
- Personalize Growth Pathways: Recognize that ambition is not monolithic. Not every team member aspires to lead a large team or climb the traditional corporate ladder. Some may find deep satisfaction in becoming a subject matter expert, a go-to technical guru. Others might be keen on mentoring, or exploring cross-functional roles. Tailor career development conversations to each individual's unique interests, strengths, and life goals. Co-create development plans rather than imposing them.
- Champion the Quiet Performers: In any team, there are those who consistently deliver excellent work without fanfare. They don't demand the spotlight, they don't frequently self-promote, but their contributions are vital. It's easy for these individuals

to be overlooked. Make a conscious effort to see them, to acknowledge their specific contributions, and to provide them with opportunities for visibility and growth. Sometimes, the most profound recognition is simply being truly seen.

Revitalizing a Team on the Brink: A Case Study in Transformation

Several years ago, I inherited a team notorious for having one of the highest attrition rates within our business unit. The atmosphere was heavy; you could almost taste the disillusionment. Trust in previous leadership was practically non-existent, and engagement was visibly, painfully absent. People came in, did the bare minimum, and watched the clock.

My first step was intensive listening. I scheduled one-on-one conversations with every single team member, creating a safe space for them to speak freely. The feedback was raw, unfiltered, and brutally honest: "We feel like interchangeable cogs in a machine," "No one here cares about what we want or what our career goals are," and "We're only ever noticed when something goes catastrophically wrong."

Armed with these insights, we initiated several key changes, none of them revolutionary, but all of them rooted in consistent care and respect:

- Fostering Connection: We established a "Fun Committee" (with rotating members to ensure diverse ideas) to organize regular, informal team connects – virtual coffee breaks, online games, themed discussions – things that helped people see each other as human beings, not just colleagues.
- Aligning Passion with Purpose: We carefully reviewed existing roles and responsibilities, looking for opportunities to realign tasks with individuals' stated interests and strengths. Where

possible, we offered stretch assignments that genuinely excited them.

- Building a Support Network: We introduced a buddy system, pairing new hires with more tenured team members, and also creating peer support pods for ongoing projects.
- Cultivating a Culture of Appreciation: We made recognition and celebration an integral part of our weekly rhythm. This wasn't just about grand gestures; it was about consistently acknowledging effort, celebrating small wins, and publicly appreciating individuals who went the extra mile.

Six months later, the transformation was remarkable. The stream of resignations had slowed to a trickle. More importantly, people were not just staying; they were showing up with renewed energy, volunteering ideas, and collaborating proactively. In a particularly heartening turn, a few team members who were already serving their notice periods approached me to withdraw their resignations. The nature of the work itself hadn't fundamentally changed. What had changed, profoundly, was their experience of doing that work.

The Alchemy of Loyalty

You cannot legislate loyalty. Employment contracts can stipulate notice periods and non-compete clauses, but they can never genuinely create a sense of belonging or inspire discretionary effort. Loyalty is not enforced; it's earned. It's an organic outcome of a healthy, nurturing environment.

When individuals feel that their voice is not just heard but genuinely matters, when they can clearly see pathways for personal and professional growth, when they know, without a shadow of a doubt, that their manager will stand by them and support them through challenging times – that is when they choose to stay. They stay not because they are obligated to, but because they want to.

Loyalty flourishes when people experience three fundamental human needs within their work environment:

- Belonging: Feeling like an accepted, respected, and integral part of a team where they can be their authentic selves.
- Growth: Perceiving that they are learning, developing new skills, and making meaningful progress in their careers.
- Respect: Knowing their contributions are valued, their opinions are considered, and they are treated with fairness and dignity.

Nurturing these elements requires time, unwavering consistency, and a high degree of emotional intelligence from leadership. But once cultivated, they create teams that are not only resilient and engaged but deeply invested in mutual success.

Embracing the Inevitable

Let's be realistic: no matter how empathetic, inspiring, and competent a manager you're, some attrition is unavoidable. Indeed, a certain degree can even be healthy for an organization. People's ambitions evolve, personal circumstances shift, and new, exciting opportunities may arise that are a better fit for their journey. Stagnation is the enemy of growth, both for individuals and organizations.

However, wise managers don't wait for the resignation letter to land on their desk before thinking about its impact. They proactively build resilient teams by:

- Cross-Skilling: Deliberately training team members in multiple roles or aspects of a project to ensure no single person is the sole repository of critical knowledge.
- Championing Documentation: Fostering a culture where processes, learnings, and project details are meticulously documented and easily accessible.
- Rotating Responsibilities: Providing opportunities for team members to take on different tasks or lead different initiatives,

which broadens their skill sets and reduces single-point dependencies.

- Maintaining Talent Pipelines: Continuously networking and identifying potential future talent, even when there is not an immediate vacancy. This includes internal talent spotting and development.

The objective is not to prevent every single departure, which is an unrealistic and even undesirable aim. The true goal is to ensure that when an exit does occur, it causes minimal disruption to the team's momentum and the organization's objectives.

Even at the highest levels of leadership, cultivating a successor, a "backup," is paramount. No leader is indispensable or should aspire to be in the same role indefinitely within an organization for its own health. Therefore, grooming the next line of leadership is a critical responsibility. Conversely, if you're in a leadership position but actively resist sharing knowledge or training others to create a dependency on yourself, it often signals deep-seated insecurity rather than irreplaceability. True value lies in empowering others, not in hoarding knowledge.

Crafting Environments Where People Choose to Flourish and Stay

Ultimately, addressing attrition effectively transcends the transactional acts of merely hiring replacements or making reactive counter-offers. It's about the proactive, continuous, and heartfelt endeavor of creating work environments where people feel genuinely inspired to stay, to contribute their best work, and to grow both personally and professionally.

Build professional relationships that extend beyond mere task allocation and deadline management. Let your team members know, through your words and actions, that they matter – not just for the outputs they produce, but for the unique individuals they are.

When your team members are deeply convinced that their growth, their well-being, and their aspirations genuinely matter to you, their commitment will transform. They will be more inclined to speak up with innovative ideas, they will demonstrate greater resilience during challenging periods, they will willingly go the extra mile, and yes, they will likely stay longer.

And even when the day comes for them to move on, as it sometimes will, they will depart with a sense of respect, carrying with them a positive impression of your leadership and a lasting connection to the team and organization – becoming advocates rather than detractors.

"In order to build a rewarding employee experience, you need to understand what matters most to your people." – Julie Bevacqua

CHAPTER 8

Psychology at Work

"Leadership is all about emotional intelligence. Management is taught, while leadership is experienced." – Rajeev Suri

Why Psychology Belongs in the Workplace

Step into the vibrant, often unpredictable ecosystem of the modern workplace. It's a space where strategies are forged, targets are chased, and innovations are born. But beneath the surface of tasks and timelines pulses a powerful, often underestimated force: human emotion. Every individual who walks through those office doors, logs into their virtual workspace, or joins that crucial meeting carries within them a universe of feelings, experiences, and inner dialogues. They bring not just their skills and expertise, but also their hopes, their anxieties, their motivations, and their unique ways of perceiving the world.

As a leader, a manager, a guide in this complex landscape, you're not orchestrating a symphony of automatons. You're navigating a delicate dance of human hearts and minds. To believe that you can effectively lead without understanding the fundamental principles of human psychology is akin to sailing uncharted waters without a compass. It's not merely beneficial to cultivate psychological insight; it's the very bedrock upon which truly impactful leadership is built. You don't need a wall full of diplomas in psychology. What you need is an insatiable curiosity about the human condition, a keen eye for observation, and a reflective spirit that constantly seeks to understand the intricate tapestry of human behavior, especially when the threads are stretched taut by pressure, frayed by uncertainty, or rewoven by change.

Unveiling the Emotional Landscape

Each member of your team navigates their professional life while simultaneously safeguarding their inner emotional world. They present a carefully constructed "professional self" – the one that delivers reports, attends meetings, and contributes to projects. But behind this facade lies a rich and often vulnerable "emotional self," filled with unspoken needs, hidden fears, and deeply held aspirations. Too often, our systems and structures focus solely on rewarding the tangible outputs of the professional self, inadvertently overlooking the subtle yet powerful influence of the emotional self.

The profound truth is this: when the emotional well-being of an individual is neglected, the vibrant energy of their professional self inevitably begins to dim. The quietude in meetings might not signify disengagement but rather a silent battle with anxiety, a fear of speaking up, or a feeling of not being heard. Resistance to new projects might not stem from laziness or defiance but from an overwhelming sense of inadequacy or a lack of clarity about the path forward. What appears as aggression or rudeness might, in reality, be a manifestation of underlying insecurity, a fear of being overlooked, or a desperate attempt to assert oneself in a perceived threat.

The pivotal moment in your journey as a leader arrives when you begin to perceive outward behavior not as an isolated problem to be fixed, but as a symptom, a signal emanating from the deeper emotional landscape of the individual. This shift in perspective fosters a leadership style imbued with compassion, understanding, and a genuine desire to support the holistic well-being of your team members.

The Unseen Barriers: Navigating the Manager's Psychological Blind Spots

Even the most well-intentioned leaders can inadvertently stumble into common psychological blind spots – ingrained assumptions that can hinder connection and impede true understanding:

- The Illusion of Assumed Agreement in Silence: How often have you heard the phrase, "Silence means yes"? In the pressured environment of a meeting, a lack of immediate verbal dissent is often misinterpreted as tacit approval. However, silence can be a sanctuary for the hesitant, the unsure, the intimidated, or simply the thoughtful individual who needs more time to process. By equating silence with agreement, we risk silencing valuable perspectives and creating an environment where genuine feedback is stifled. True engagement requires actively soliciting diverse viewpoints, creating space for thoughtful reflection, and ensuring everyone feels empowered to voice their opinions, even if they differ from the prevailing view.

- The Myth of Uniform Fairness: The desire for fairness is noble, but its misapplication lies in the assumption that treating everyone the same equates to treating everyone equitably. Human beings are wonderfully diverse, each possessing a unique constellation of needs, learning styles, communication preferences, and motivational drivers. To apply a one-size-fits-all approach in the name of fairness is to ignore this fundamental truth. True equity lies in recognizing and responding to the individual needs of each team member, providing tailored support, and fostering an environment where everyone has the opportunity to thrive, even if their paths and requirements differ.

- The Fallacy of Pure Willpower in Performance: While dedication and effort are undoubtedly crucial for achieving goals, attributing performance solely to willpower overlooks the complex interplay of factors that influence an individual's ability to succeed.

Emotional well-being, clarity of expectations, access to resources, supportive relationships, and a sense of psychological safety all play significant roles. To believe that performance is simply a matter of someone "wanting it enough" can lead to frustration, judgment, and a failure to address underlying obstacles that may be hindering an individual's progress.

- The Invisibility of Stress and Effort: We often celebrate visible outcomes – the completed project, the successful sale, the tangible result. However, we frequently fail to acknowledge the invisible yet significant emotional and mental effort that precedes these achievements. The late nights fueled by anxiety, the careful navigation of interpersonal conflicts, the quiet perseverance through challenging setbacks – these often go unnoticed and unrewarded. By focusing solely on visible outcomes, we risk creating a culture that undervalues the emotional labor and resilience that are essential for sustained success and individual well-being.

- The Dismissal of Emotional Intelligence as a "Soft" Skill: For too long, emotional intelligence has been relegated to the realm of "soft skills," deemed secondary to technical prowess and strategic thinking. This is a profound misconception. Emotional intelligence – the ability to understand and manage one's own emotions and to recognize and influence the emotions of others – is not a peripheral attribute of good leadership; it's the very core. It underpins effective communication, conflict resolution, team cohesion, and the ability to inspire and motivate others. To consider it optional is to fundamentally misunderstand the human element that drives organizational success.

These blind spots are not indictments of your character; they are inherent limitations of the human experience. Recognizing them, however, is the crucial first step towards evolving your leadership, fostering deeper connections, and unlocking the full potential of your team.

Building the Foundation of Trust

Psychological safety is not about creating a perpetually comfortable or conflict-free environment. It's about cultivating a deep-seated trust within the team – the unwavering belief that individuals can express their thoughts, admit their mistakes, and share their innovative ideas without fear of ridicule, punishment, or negative repercussions.

In teams where psychological safety thrives, a palpable sense of openness permeates the atmosphere. People feel empowered to take calculated risks, to ask clarifying questions without feeling inadequate, and to openly admit, "I don't know," without fearing judgment. Conversely, in environments where psychological safety is absent, a culture of silence prevails. Individuals hesitate to speak up, even when they foresee potential problems, fearing that their vulnerability will be met with criticism or blame. Innovation is stifled, mistakes are hidden, and the collective intelligence of the team remains untapped.

As a leader, the responsibility for nurturing psychological safety rests squarely upon your shoulders. You cultivate this vital foundation through deliberate actions and consistent behaviors:

- Actively Inviting Diverse Opinions and Constructive Dissent: Create explicit opportunities for all voices to be heard, even those that challenge the prevailing view. Encourage healthy debate and demonstrate that differing perspectives are valued as opportunities for learning and growth.
- Demonstrating Humility by Acknowledging Your Own Mistakes: Leading with vulnerability is a powerful way to build trust. When you openly admit your own errors, you create a culture where imperfection is accepted as a natural part of the learning process, and others feel safer to acknowledge their own missteps.
- Responding to Feedback with Openness and Without Defensiveness: When team members offer feedback, even if it's critical, receive it with grace and a genuine desire to understand

their perspective. Avoid becoming defensive or dismissive, as this will quickly shut down future communication.

- Protecting Your Team from Humiliation and Blame: Stand as a shield for your team, especially when external pressures or mistakes occur. Focus on collective learning and problem-solving rather than assigning individual blame. Ensure that mistakes are viewed as opportunities for improvement, not as grounds for public shaming.

Building psychological safety is not a one-time initiative; it's an ongoing commitment woven into the fabric of every interaction. It's nurtured in every conversation where a team member feels truly seen, genuinely heard, and respectfully valued.

Consider my own experience with a particularly demanding client. Their relentless pressure stemmed from a perceived overcommitment on our part, leading to unrealistic expectations and a trickle-down effect of immense stress throughout the team. The atmosphere became so toxic that team members, including supervisors and managers, began experiencing nightmares. It was in this deeply concerning environment that the urgent need for psychological safety became starkly apparent.

I connected with the team of supervisors and managers, providing a safe space for them to articulate their concerns. They openly shared the multitude of issues they were facing. While I acknowledged the professional growth that can arise from navigating challenging client relationships, I also validated their feelings, acknowledged instances where our initial assessment might have been flawed, and identified areas where we could have better advocated for the team. Crucially, I immediately escalated their feedback to my senior leadership.

We did not expect an overnight resolution. However, the immediate impact was profound. The team understood that their struggles were being acknowledged, their voices were being heard, and their concerns were being addressed at the highest level. This simple act of validation and escalation instilled a renewed sense of confidence and trust, demonstrating that their well-being was a priority.

I must mention 1 more incident here. It was back in March 2020. The world outside had shrunk to the confines of our homes. An unnerving quiet had descended upon the streets, but in our makeshift home offices, a storm was brewing. The global pandemic had not only locked us down but had also exposed the raw vulnerabilities in our infrastructure. Client escalations, already a source of anxiety, began to multiply at an alarming rate, each one a fresh wave threatening to pull us under. The pressure was immense, a relentless vice squeezing the air from our lungs. Team meetings, once collaborative spaces, became battlegrounds. Frayed nerves led to sharp words, frustration boiled over into finger-pointing, and the very fabric of our team felt like it was tearing apart under the strain. Each of us felt isolated, overwhelmed, and the collective weight of expectation was crushing.

It was amidst this escalating crisis, during a particularly fraught period, that Mr. Ramanarayana Parhi intervened. I remember it was a call scheduled quite late in the evening, a time when exhaustion typically gnawed at our resolve, and the dim glow of our laptop screens felt like the only light in a shrinking world. The atmosphere on that call was thick with unspoken tensions, the residue of earlier disagreements hanging heavy in the virtual air.

Then, Mr. Parhi spoke. His voice, calm yet resonant, cut through the static of our collective stress. I will never forget his words, nor the profound stillness that followed them.

"Guys," he began, his tone steady and empathetic, acknowledging the weariness he must have sensed in all of us. "We have a big challenge ahead. There is no denying that." He paused, letting the reality of our situation settle without adding to its weight. Then, he continued, "Just do whatever is possible from your side. Focus on what you can control, give it your best, but please, don't take so much stress upon yourselves that it breaks you."

This alone would have been a comfort, a much-needed permission to be human in an inhuman situation. But what he said next was what truly shifted the earth beneath our feet.

"We will deal with the client," he stated, a quiet assurance in his voice. "And if it comes to it, if anyone has to take the blame for any shortcomings, I will myself let the client know that I am the one who failed in meeting their expectations."

Silence. The kind of silence that is not empty, but full – full of shock, then dawning respect, and finally, an overwhelming sense of relief. In that single, selfless declaration, Mr. Parhi had offered himself as a shield. He wasn't just a manager delegating tasks; he was a leader prepared to stand in the line of fire for his team. He did not just ask us to face the storm; he stood before us, ready to bear its brunt.

The impact was instantaneous and transformative. It was as if a heavy, invisible burden had been lifted from our collective shoulders. The internal strife, the blame, the crippling fear of failure – it all seemed to dissipate in the warmth of his extraordinary commitment. What bloomed in its place was a profound sense of trust, not just in him, but in each other. We were no longer a fractured group of individuals struggling in isolation; we were a team, united by a leader who had shown us what true support looked like.

That night, something changed within each of us. The exhaustion did not magically vanish, nor did the challenges evaporate. But our approach was revolutionized. Fueled by a renewed sense of purpose and an almost fierce loyalty, everyone started pouring their energy, not just 100%, but what felt like 200%, into their work. It wasn't driven by fear of reprimand, but by a deep-seated desire to honor the faith Mr. Parhi had placed in us, to ensure his sacrifice wouldn't be necessary. We wanted to make things right, not just for the client, but for him.

And remarkably, with this rekindled spirit and collaborative energy, things began to turn around. We found creative solutions, supported each other through the technical glitches, and collectively navigated the complexities of our clients' demands. The path was still arduous, but we walked it together, buoyed by the incredible foundation of trust Mr. Parhi had laid down with his words on that unforgettable evening. It was a masterclass in leadership, a moment that demonstrated how true strength lies not in demanding results, but in inspiring dedication through empathy and courageous accountability.

Emotional Intelligence at the Helm of Leadership

Emotional intelligence (EQ) is often misconstrued as mere niceness or agreeableness. In reality, it's a far more profound and powerful attribute. It's the capacity for acute awareness – of your own internal emotional landscape and the nuanced emotional states of those around you – coupled with the ability to respond thoughtfully and effectively in interpersonal interactions.

For leaders, four key dimensions of EQ are particularly critical:

- Self-awareness: This is the foundational pillar of EQ – the ability to recognize and understand your own emotions, triggers, moods, and behavioral patterns. It involves an honest appraisal of your strengths and weaknesses and an understanding of how your emotions impact your decisions and interactions.
- Self-regulation: This dimension encompasses your ability to manage your own emotions effectively, particularly in the face of pressure or adversity. It involves staying calm under fire, avoiding impulsive or reactive behaviors, and maintaining composure even in challenging situations.
- Empathy: Empathy is the capacity to understand and share the feelings of others. It involves stepping into someone else's shoes, recognizing their emotional state without judgment, and

acknowledging their perspective, even if you don't necessarily agree with it.

- Relationship Management: This encompasses the skills needed to navigate interpersonal interactions effectively. It includes the ability to manage conflict constructively, deliver and receive feedback with grace, foster collaboration, inspire and influence others, and build strong, meaningful relationships.

While intellectual prowess (IQ) may often pave the way for individuals to ascend the leadership ladder, it's emotional intelligence that sustains long-term success and fosters truly impactful leadership. Personally, I have come to rely more heavily on the insights and guidance of my EQ than on pure intellectual analysis. It's the emotional connection, the intuitive understanding of human dynamics, that often guides the most effective and meaningful actions.

Deciphering the Unspoken Language: Reading Between the Lines

Psychological insight transcends the literal words spoken. It involves a keen awareness of what is not being said, the subtle nuances of how something is said, and the timing of its delivery. These nonverbal cues often reveal the underlying emotional currents that words alone cannot express.

As a leader, cultivating the ability to "read between the lines" can provide invaluable insights into the true state of your team. Be attuned to subtle signals that might indicate underlying emotional distress:

- The Perpetual "Fine" Accompanied by Averted Gaze: A team member who consistently responds with a curt "fine" while avoiding eye contact might be signaling discomfort, anxiety, or a desire to disengage from further inquiry.
- The Laughter that Masks Dejection: Someone who laughs off criticism in a meeting but then becomes withdrawn and silent

afterwards might be masking feelings of hurt, shame, or a sense of being undermined.

- **The Sudden Shift from Enthusiasm to Quietude:** An employee who was once vibrant and engaged but suddenly becomes quiet and withdrawn in meetings might be experiencing burnout, discouragement, or a personal struggle that is impacting their professional demeanor.
- **The High Performer with Slipping Standards:** A consistently reliable individual who starts missing minor deadlines or exhibiting uncharacteristic errors might be grappling with overwhelm, stress, or a decline in motivation.

These are not mere personality quirks to be dismissed. They are emotional signals, subtle cries for attention and understanding. You don't necessarily need to launch an immediate intervention, but you do need to acknowledge these cues and gently explore the underlying causes through genuine care, thoughtful curiosity, and a desire to connect on a human level.

The Art of Adaptability: Managing the Mosaic of Personalities

Every team is a rich and dynamic tapestry woven from diverse personality types. You'll encounter introverts who draw energy from solitude and reflection, and extroverts who thrive in social interaction. You'll work with analytical thinkers who prioritize logic and data, and empathetic feelers who are deeply attuned to emotions and values. Some individuals will be naturally assertive, readily taking initiative, while others will be more accommodating, prioritizing harmony and collaboration.

In this diverse landscape, a rigid, one-size-fits-all approach to leadership is destined to fall short. What motivates and empowers one individual may demotivate and disengage another.

Your role as a leader is not to mold everyone into a uniform shape but to become a flexible and adaptable guide. Some team members will flourish with clear structure, detailed checklists, and well-defined processes. Others will thrive on autonomy, creative freedom, and the ability to chart their own course. Some will need frequent reassurance and positive reinforcement, while others will respond best to direct, honest feedback.

Adapting your communication style, your support mechanisms, and your motivational approaches to align with the individual needs and preferences of your team members is not favoritism; it's the very essence of psychological intelligence in action. It demonstrates that you see them, you understand them, and you value their unique contributions.

I have personally faced accusations of favoritism, particularly regarding my communication style with certain individuals. This feedback prompted a period of intense self-reflection. While it's impossible to control others' perceptions, I came to realize that my seemingly different approaches were rooted in an attempt to connect with each individual in a way that resonated with their personality and needs.

For instance, I had a highly talented supervisor in my team who possessed a fiery temperament and reacted strongly to feedback. While her performance was consistently excellent, navigating difficult conversations required a delicate touch. I learned that the most effective approach was to listen patiently to her perspective, allowing her to fully express her thoughts before offering my own input or suggestions. This approach often diffused her initial frustration, and she became more receptive to constructive feedback. To some observers, my patient demeanor might have appeared as preferential treatment, but it was simply an application of psychological intelligence – adapting my communication style to effectively engage with her unique personality.

This same principle extends beyond the workplace. My family has often playfully labeled me a workaholic, citing my limited availability. However, I've found that patiently listening to their concerns, allowing them to fully express their feelings without interruption, often proves to be the most effective way to foster understanding and connection.

It's crucial to note, however, that while adaptability and empathy are paramount, these qualities must be tempered with unwavering integrity. When faced with ethical breaches or issues of integrity, your emotional responses must align with your principles, providing you with the strength and clarity to act decisively and justly, regardless of individual personalities or relationships.

The Silent Saboteurs: How Unresolved Emotions Undermine Performance

The notion that individuals can compartmentalize their lives, leaving their emotions at the doorstep when they enter the workplace, is a dangerous fallacy. Unprocessed frustrations, lingering shame, underlying fears, and pervasive insecurities are not simply left behind; they are carried within, silently sabotaging focus, motivation, and ultimately, performance.

A team member who consistently feels unappreciated will eventually withdraw their discretionary effort, no longer going the extra mile. Someone who harbors a deep-seated fear of failure will shy away from challenging opportunities, limiting their growth and contribution. An individual who feels consistently unheard and undervalued will gradually disengage, their passion and commitment eroding over time.

As a leader, you're not expected to be a therapist, diagnosing and resolving every personal struggle. However, you have a responsibility to create a work environment where these underlying emotional struggles can be acknowledged without judgment. By fostering a culture of empathy and understanding, you create space for vulnerability and open communication, which can be the first step towards addressing these silent saboteurs of performance.

The Invisible Burden: The Silent Influence of Mental Health

Mental health in the workplace is no longer a peripheral concern; it's a central factor influencing productivity, engagement, and overall well-being. Issues such as burnout, anxiety, imposter syndrome, and chronic stress are not abstract concepts; they are tangible realities that affect individuals at all levels, including managers themselves.

Creating a culture where mental wellness is normalized is not just a compassionate act; it's a strategic imperative. Regularly check in with your team members, not just on their tasks and deadlines, but also on their energy levels, their focus, and their overall well-being. Encourage the utilization of mental health days without stigma, reinforcing the message that prioritizing mental health is a sign of strength, not weakness. If you observe a sudden and significant drop in a team member's performance, approach the situation with concern and empathy, rather than jumping to negative assumptions.

You don't need to be a mental health professional, but you can be a safe and supportive presence, someone your team members feel comfortable talking to when they are struggling.

In recent times, I've observed a growing trend among younger professionals citing mental health challenges as significant obstacles in their work lives. While acknowledging the validity of these struggles, my observations have also led me to believe that a significant contributor to workplace mental health issues in today's world is the pervasive nature of distraction. As Cal Newport astutely points out in his book Deep Work, "Focus helps employees find meaning; distraction fuels dissatisfaction." Recognizing this connection, I personally conducted a session within my organization on the principles and practices of deep work. Even if this initiative positively impacted the mindset of just one individual, I would consider it a meaningful success. By fostering a culture of focused work and mindful engagement, we can begin to mitigate the distractions that often contribute to stress and dissatisfaction.

Cultivating Your Own Psychological Awareness

True leadership doesn't commence with mastering external strategies or market dynamics; it originates in the often-unexplored landscape of your own mind and emotions. Before you can hope to effectively guide, inspire, or support others, you must embark on the crucial journey of understanding yourself. This is not mere navel-gazing; it's the foundational work of impactful leadership.

Begin by becoming a keen observer of your internal reactions. Ask yourself with genuine curiosity:

- What specific scenarios, interactions, or pressures tend to ignite frustration, impatience, or defensiveness within me? Pinpointing these triggers is like mapping the fault lines in your emotional terrain – knowing where they are allows you to anticipate tremors and respond with intention, not just instinct.
- When engaged in conversation, particularly during disagreements or high-stakes discussions, is my primary goal to truly absorb the other person's viewpoint, their underlying feelings, and their unspoken needs? Or do I find myself mentally rehearsing my counter-argument, waiting for a pause simply to deploy my own perspective? Shifting from listening-to-reply to listening-to-comprehend unlocks deeper connection and understanding.
- How do I genuinely process setbacks? When faced with failure – whether my own misstep or a team member's – is my immediate reaction one of learning, adaptation, and forward momentum, or does it veer towards blame, justification, or withdrawal? Your

response to adversity sets a powerful tone for resilience and psychological safety.

- When someone expresses strong emotions – be it anxiety, disappointment, or even excitement – is my impulse to immediately offer solutions, downplay their feelings, or steer the conversation back to 'practicalities'? Or can I consciously create a space for those emotions to simply be, offering validation and presence before jumping to 'fix-it' mode? Allowing emotional room is a profound act of respect and support.

Developing this profound self-awareness is not just a helpful trait; it's the bedrock upon which resonant leadership is built. The more intimately you understand your own emotional patterns, biases, and responses, the more attuned you become to the subtle currents of emotion in others. You develop an intuitive compass for navigating the complexities of human interaction.

Practical Practices for Everyday Psychological Leadership

Integrating this awareness doesn't require a radical, overnight transformation of your leadership persona. Instead, think of it as weaving stronger, more empathetic threads into the existing fabric of your interactions. Start with small, consistent practices:

- Initiate Meetings with Presence: Beyond the agenda, consider starting team gatherings or one-on-ones with a brief, voluntary check-in. Asking "How's everyone arriving today?" or "What's one feeling present in the room?" can normalize emotional expression and create a more human-centered atmosphere.
- Embrace the Power of the Pause: In moments charged with tension or high emotion, train yourself to resist the urge for an immediate reaction. Take a conscious breath. This small gap creates a crucial buffer between stimulus and response, allowing you to choose a more thoughtful, less reactive course of action.

- Inquire Before Intervening: When a team member seems stressed, stuck, or upset, resist the urge to immediately prescribe solutions based on your assumptions. Instead, ask empowering questions like, "What support would be most helpful to you right now?" or "What do you need from me, or the team, in this situation?" This conveys trust and ensures your support is genuinely useful.

- Acknowledge the Unseen Effort: Look beyond just the measurable outcomes and deliverables. Make a conscious effort to recognize and appreciate the emotional labor involved in work – the courage it took to voice a dissenting opinion, the patience demonstrated during a frustrating process, the kindness shown to a struggling colleague, the resilience displayed after a setback. Celebrating these qualities reinforces the values you wish to cultivate. Dr. Manoj Naik exemplified this: though we never worked directly, he consistently affirmed my efforts and those of everyone he met, even when outcomes weren't perfect. His approach showed the power of recognizing dedication itself to foster encouragement and loyalty.

Remember, the enduring impact of your leadership is not solely defined by quarterly reports or project milestones. It's profoundly shaped by the cumulative effect of daily interactions – by how valued, understood, and psychologically safe people feel when working alongside you.

Lead the Mind to Win the Heart

Let's be clear: delving into the psychological dimension of leadership is not a 'soft' detour from the 'real' business of leading. It's the real business. It confronts the most challenging aspects of the role precisely because it deals with the invisible, dynamic, and deeply personal nature of human beings. It acknowledges that we lead whole people, not just skill sets or job titles.

When you begin to consciously view your team not merely as resources executing tasks, but as individuals with unique emotional landscapes, motivations, fears, and aspirations, a fundamental shift occurs. Your interactions gain depth and authenticity. Conflicts, while still inevitable, tend to de-escalate more quickly and become opportunities for mutual understanding rather than entrenched battles. Your ability to truly influence – to inspire commitment rather than mere compliance – expands organically.

This path is not just about managing others more effectively; it's a journey of mutual growth. By attuning to the psychological needs of your team, you inevitably deepen your own emotional intelligence and capacity for connection. You move beyond simply directing people; you actively participate in their development, and in doing so, you evolve yourself. Leading the mind, through understanding and empathy, is the surest way to truly connect with the human heart and unlock collective potential.

> *"Convince people and you win their minds. Inspire people and you win their hearts." – Ron Kaufman*

Part III

Performance and Feedback

Chapter 9

Performance Management with a Human Lens

"The most effective problem is that performance appraisals often don't accurately assess performance." – W. Edwards Deming

What Performance Management Really Means

When the words "performance management" echo through the corporate hallways, what's the first image that flashes in our minds? For too many, it's the sterile chill of a rating spreadsheet, the looming deadline of goal submissions, the forced formality of a year-end appraisal that feels more like a verdict than a conversation. We picture a season, a cycle, an obligation. But this, my friends, is merely the ghost of what performance management should be.

True performance management is not a date on the calendar; it's the daily breath of a thriving team. It's an unending dialogue, a commitment woven into the fabric of every interaction. It's the patient art of illuminating the path ahead, of whispering encouragement when the journey gets steep, of championing growth not just for the bottom line, but for the individual spirit. It's about building a bridge of understanding between the organization's aspirations and the employee's own unfolding story.

Imagine a space where success is not a secret code but a shared vision, painted with such clarity that everyone sees their unique brushstroke contributing to the masterpiece. This is performance management done with heart. It's not about wielding a red pen to circle flaws; it's about offering a steady hand, a knowing glance that says, "I see your potential, and I'm here to help you unleash it, consistently and with a confidence that radiates from within."

Beyond the Bell Curve's Shadow

Traditional systems, with their heavy reliance on numerical ratings and forced rankings, often cast a long, cold shadow. They promise objectivity but frequently deliver anxiety, fostering a quiet undercurrent of competition where collaboration should bloom. Measurement, undeniably, has its place. We need markers to understand progress. But when the system becomes so obsessed with the metric that it forgets the human, it loses its soul. Can a year of tireless effort, of late nights fueled by passion, of creative breakthroughs born from sheer persistence, truly be distilled into a single digit or a predetermined slot on a bell curve?

Performance is not a flat, static score; it's a rich, evolving narrative. It's a tapestry woven with threads of resilience in the face of setbacks, the quiet courage to try something new, the sweat of genuine effort, the lessons learned from missteps, and the exhilarating spark of growth. A manager who truly manages performance doesn't just glance at the final output. They lean in, seeking to understand the how behind the what. They explore the terrain the employee traversed, the hidden obstacles they surmounted, the dormant strengths they awakened along the way.

I've sat in too many rooms, a silent observer to the palpable discomfort of supervisors fumbling for words, unable to connect the performance rating they've delivered to the reality of their subordinate's contributions. The air grows thick with unspoken truths. And then comes the all-too-common escape hatch: "You know, I pushed for a higher rating, but leadership... well, they had to normalize it." It's a fragile shield, and it shatters trust. Even if the hierarchical pressures are real, a true leader finds a way to ground their feedback in observable data, in the transparent logic of organizational needs, or even the sometimes unpalatable rationale of a bell curve, if explained with empathy and honesty.

Conversely, when a team member shines brightly, how often do these same managers, quick to deflect blame, readily bask in the reflected glory, conveniently forgetting to acknowledge the supportive endorsements they received from their own superiors? These are often the leaders who enter performance discussions unprepared, their folders empty of data, their minds devoid of specific examples. They shy away from the deep, sometimes challenging, one-on-one connections where real performance dialogue happens. This avoidance is not just a missed opportunity; it's the breeding ground for a culture of cynicism and disengagement. Performance dialogue must be a constant, living thing, not a dreaded annual autopsy. It's the manager's solemn duty to offer feedback that flows like a steady stream, not a once-a-year tidal wave, to extend a helping hand proactively, because managing performance is not about manipulating numbers; it's about nurturing human beings, with all their complex, vibrant, and sometimes vulnerable emotions.

When we dare to shift our perspective from one of detached judgment to one of committed partnership, the entire dynamic transforms. Performance conversations cease to be interrogations and blossom into empowering, honest, and truly constructive exchanges.

Illuminating the Path: Setting Expectations with Clarity and Heart

One of the most profound, yet frequently underestimated, pillars of effective performance management is the art of setting expectations. So many managers operate under the dangerous illusion that their team inherently "gets it," that the targets and standards are universally understood. But assumptions are the termites of alignment, silently eating away at the foundations of good work.

Crystal-clear expectations transcend mere task lists and deadlines. They paint a vivid picture of how work should be approached – the collaborative spirit, the ethical considerations, the innovative mindset. They define what true excellence looks like, not just in outcome but in conduct. They articulate the behaviors that breathe life into team values. Critically, they establish how success will be recognized and measured, leaving no room for ambiguity. A well-crafted goal is not just a sentence in a performance document; it's a pact, a shared compass that orients every individual effort towards a common horizon, creating focus and invigorating alignment.

The most agile and successful teams don't set expectations once and then carve them in stone. They treat them as living agreements, revisiting and refining them as the landscape of work shifts, as roles evolve, as new challenges emerge. Clarity, like a well-tended garden, requires constant maintenance.

The Rhythm of Growth: Ongoing Conversation, Not the Annual Ritual

As I've emphasized, performance conversations should never feel like a surprise party where the guest of honor is ambushed. By the time a formal review period arrives, it should be a confirmation, a summary of dialogues that have been happening all along. There should be no shocking revelations, no unexpected critiques.

Imagine a rhythm of regular check-ins, impromptu feedback moments, and informal coaching huddles. These aren't burdensome additions to a manager's schedule; they are investments in clarity and confidence. These touchpoints are the lifeblood of reflective practice, helping individuals see where they are soaring, where they are meeting the mark, and where gentle course correction or further development could unlock new levels of achievement. Without this steady drumbeat of communication, formal reviews inevitably become fraught with tension, defensiveness, and missed opportunities for genuine connection.

Truly skilled manager weaves performance feedback into the daily tapestry of interactions. They create pockets of psychological safety where questions like, "How are you feeling about your progress on this project?" or "Is there anything standing in your way, anything I can help remove so you can do your best work?" can be asked and answered with candor. These simple inquiries are potent builders of trust; they open channels for dialogue and enable adjustments long before minor eddies become major whirlpools. But let's be honest: how many managers consistently cultivate this environment? The answer, too often, is "not enough."

Managing Underperformance with Compassion and Courage

Addressing underperformance is, without a doubt, one of the most challenging terrains a manager must navigate. It's tempting, perhaps even a natural human defense, to quickly label someone as "not cutting it" or "a poor performer." But beneath every dip in performance, every missed target, lies a story, a reason – sometimes rooted in personal struggles, sometimes entangled in organizational complexities, sometimes a simple mismatch of skill and role.

Is it a lack of clarity in the expectations set? Is there a silent cry for more support or resources? Could personal stressors be casting a long shadow over their work life? Is disengagement a symptom of a deeper misalignment? Or is it, perhaps, that their unique talents are simply not the right fit for the current demands? Before any judgment is cast, before any action is taken, the unwavering first step must always be a conversation – one initiated with genuine curiosity, not veiled accusation. Seek to understand the landscape from their perspective before you begin to assess the situation.

Imagine opening with, "I've noticed a few things that concern me regarding [specific examples], and I genuinely want to understand how things are going for you, from your point of view." This is not a confrontation; it's an invitation. It unlocks the door to an honest exchange, allowing the root causes to surface. Once that understanding is established, a path forward can be co-created. This might involve targeted support, intensive coaching, a reassignment of tasks, or, in some cases, a thoughtful reassessment of the role itself.

Holding someone accountable for their performance doesn't necessitate harshness, criticism, or blame. It demands unwavering honesty, consistent follow-through, and a commitment to fairness.

Yet, we see it time and again: managers who eagerly step into the limelight to claim the successes of their high-flyers, but who vanish into the shadows when confronted with underperformance within their ranks. When questioned, the defensive refrain often surfaces: "What miracles do you expect me to perform with the resources I've been given?" This is not leadership; it's an abdication of responsibility. The true test of a manager lies in their commitment to those who are struggling. It's about meticulously understanding the gaps, co-creating a clear, supportive glide path for improvement, and acting as an unwavering pillar of support, offering both challenge and encouragement in equal measure.

Several years ago, I was part of a project launch where the team, despite its potential, was faltering significantly. Yes, there was a palpable knowledge gap, but more troublingly, a pervasive apathy had set in; the spark of curiosity, the willingness to learn, seemed extinguished. In an attempt to address this, a townhall was convened, and a very senior leader was invited to speak. Instead of seeking to understand the team's pain points or the undercurrents of their disengagement, this leader delivered a series of remarks that landed like stones, creating ripples of resentment that quickly escalated into a significant spike in attrition. It was a painful lesson in how not to motivate. However, what followed was a quiet testament to the power of compassionate leadership. The remaining team members, along with supportive line managers, rallied. We leaned into each other, fostering an environment of mutual support, open communication, and shared learning. With more compassion, more patience, and a collective will to succeed, that same team underwent a remarkable transformation in under six months, exceeding all expectations. The senior leader who had spoken so dismissively was no longer with the organization to witness this turnaround, but I often think that had that person seen it, would have felt an immense sense of pride – and perhaps, a valuable lesson learned.

The Radiance of Recognition

While addressing underperformance is a critical responsibility, the power of timely, genuine recognition is its equally crucial, and often tragically neglected, counterpart.

Human beings are wired for connection and acknowledgment. We don't just desire to be seen; we thrive when our efforts are noticed, when our contributions are valued. When individuals feel that their hard work, their creativity, their dedication is genuinely acknowledged, they don't just meet expectations; they invest more of their discretionary energy, more of their authentic selves, into their work. Recognition doesn't always require grand gestures or elaborate ceremonies. Sometimes, the most potent acknowledgments are the simple, sincere ones: a handwritten note, a specific compliment in a team meeting, or a quick message saying, "The way you navigated that difficult client conversation was brilliant – thank you." These moments can illuminate someone's entire week, reinforcing their value and their impact.

The magic ingredients are timeliness, specificity, and sincerity. Recognition shouldn't be hoarded for the annual awards banquet; it should be woven into the daily rhythm of leadership, a natural expression of appreciation for a job well done, for effort demonstrated, for values lived.

When people know, deep in their core, that their good work will be seen and appreciated, a subtle but powerful shift occurs. They begin to actively seek out opportunities to contribute further, to innovate, to excel. They become partners in their own success and the success of the team.

I vividly recall a period around 2009-2010, when I was a dedicated team member at Quintiles (now Iqvia). I was deeply immersed in my work, driven by an internal desire to contribute my best, and by all accounts, I was performing at a very high level within the pharmacovigilance department. One Friday, I remember a surge of focused energy; I had managed to process a record number of transactions, setting new personal and perhaps even departmental highs for a single day and week. To be honest, I wasn't seeking any reward; the satisfaction of the work itself was compelling. But then, something unexpected happened. My manager at the time, Tripti, along with several other managers, approached my desk with a certificate of achievement. The surprise and warmth of that gesture filled me with an immense sense of happiness and pride. A few hours later, an email landed in everyone's inbox from my super manager, Dr. Naveen KK. He highlighted my achievement, holding it up not just as a record, but as an example of dedication and quality for the entire team to aspire to. That public acknowledgment, that framing of my effort as a role model, did something profound. It wasn't just about the pride, though that was certainly there. It instilled in me an even deeper sense of ownership, a quiet resolve that this level of commitment was now my baseline, that I had a standard to uphold, not out of pressure, but out of a desire to continue earning that trust and respect. More than fifteen years have passed since that day, but the echo of that recognition, and the sense of ownership it ignited, remains a powerful motivator within me. Recognition, delivered at the right moment, with genuine intent, is not just a pat on the back; it's an investment in future commitment.

Cultivating Potential: Growing Performance, Not Just Grading It

The soul of performance management, its most transformative power, lies in its developmental capacity, not merely its evaluative function. The crucial shift in mindset is from asking, "Why did not you deliver more?" to sincerely inquiring, "How can we, together, help you grow and achieve even greater things?"

This single change in approach can revolutionize the entire tone and texture of the relationship between a manager and their team members. Where fear of judgment once resided, trust begins to blossom. Where reluctant compliance was the norm, enthusiastic commitment takes root.

Great managers understand that performance discussions, even the formal ones, are prime opportunities for fostering growth. They don't just present scores; they explore aspirations. They ask about learning goals; about skills the employee wishes to acquire or hone. They deliver feedback that is designed to build up, not to bruise egos – feedback that is specific, actionable, and future-focused. They act as connectors, recommending resources, suggesting mentors, or identifying projects that will stretch individuals in ways that align with their potential and their ambitions.

Viewed through this lens, performance management ceases to be a dreaded grading system and evolves into a dynamic, energizing growth engine for both the individual and the organization.

The Art of Unlocking: Coaching for Impact

Performance coaching is not a remedial measure reserved for high-potentials or those on formal development plans. It's a universal tool, a way of interacting that benefits everyone on the team, every single day.

Often, the chasm between a struggling employee and a thriving one is not a deficiency in capability, but a deficit in confidence, a lack of clarity, or the absence of insightful coaching. A manager who coaches effectively doesn't just provide answers; they ask powerful, thought-provoking questions. "If you were to approach this challenge without any fear of failure, what might you do differently?" or "Looking back at that situation, what's one key learning you can carry forward?" These aren't questions with right or wrong answers; they are invitations to introspection, to self-awareness, and to taking ownership of one's own developmental journey.

Coaching is not about dictating solutions from on high. It's about creating a fertile space where individuals can unearth their own insights, devise their own strategies, and ultimately, discover the path to their own success.

I once had the profound privilege of working under the leadership of Shri K V Subramaniam, the former CEO and President of Reliance Life Sciences. Our team had weekly performance review meetings with him, and these were unlike any I had experienced before or since. He had this incredible knack for transforming every review into a subtle coaching session. He wouldn't just review numbers; he would engage us in a dialogue that invariably left us with "food for thought" – new perspectives, challenging questions, or unexplored avenues that we would then be eager to investigate before our next meeting. His style was unique; there was never a sense of pressure or direct command. Instead, he exuded a quiet confidence in us, making us believe we could find the answers. Two practices of KVS Sir stand out vividly in my memory. One was his innovative use of a "Journal Club." This wasn't just about discussing scientific papers; it was a masterclass in indirect coaching, a forum where he skillfully guided us to sharpen our presentation skills, our analytical thinking, and our ability to articulate complex ideas concisely across a multitude of topics. The second was his unwavering belief in people, demonstrated by his willingness to entrust us with additional responsibilities, often stretching us beyond our perceived limits, thereby signaling his confidence in our capacity to grow and succeed. He did not just manage performance; he cultivated it.

The Symphony of Success: Balancing the Collective and the Individual

While performance is so often measured and rewarded at the individual level, its true genesis is almost always collective. In the intricate dance of modern work, particularly within teams, success is rarely a solo act. It's the product of seamless collaboration, unwavering mutual support, and a deeply ingrained sense of shared accountability.

As a manager, it's therefore paramount to develop an eye not just for individual brilliance, but also for those often quieter, yet equally vital, behaviors that uplift the entire team. Consider the colleague who generously shares their knowledge to help a struggling peer catch up, the experienced team member who volunteers to mentor a newcomer, patiently guiding them through the initial learning curve, or the individual who instinctively steps forward to shoulder extra burdens during a crisis. These contributions are the glue that binds a team, the oil that smooths its operations, yet they often don't appear as neat line items on a KPI spreadsheet.

Striving for a harmonious balance between individual goals and the overall health and cohesion of the team is essential for sustainable, long-term performance. It fosters an environment where people are more inclined to collaborate with, rather than compete against, each other, creating a rising tide that lifts all boats.

A Single Conversation That Shifted My Perspective

Some years ago, I had the opportunity to manage a young associate named Subhradeep. He was exceptionally intelligent, highly disciplined, and possessed a strong technical skillset. Yet, despite these qualities, his performance reviews, after an initial promising period, consistently plateaued at "good." He was solid, reliable, but somehow never quite broke through to "great." There was an invisible ceiling.

When I became his manager, one of my first priorities was to understand this discrepancy. I invited him for an extended, informal conversation, creating a space where he might feel comfortable sharing more than just project updates. As we talked, the pieces began to fall into place. Subhradeep, it turned out, harbored a deep-seated lack of confidence when it came to speaking up in client meetings, even when he had valuable insights. He also confessed to a strong hesitation in asking for help or clarification, fearing it would make him appear incompetent or weak.

My mind immediately flashed back to the wisdom of KVS Sir and his concept of the Journal Club – creating safe spaces for skill development. Inspired by this, I formulated a gentle, supportive plan for Subhradeep. I introduced him to the local Toastmasters chapter, knowing it would provide a structured, encouraging environment to build his communication and public speaking confidence. Simultaneously, within our team meetings, and especially in client-facing situations, I made a conscious effort to create opportunities for him to speak, ensuring he knew it was a safe space to contribute, even if his initial contributions were brief. I'd often gently prompt him, "Subhradeep, you had some interesting thoughts on this in our earlier discussion, would you mind sharing?" Within three months, the transformation was palpable. His shoulders seemed broader, his voice clearer, his contributions more frequent and insightful.

By the end of that performance year, Subhradeep wasn't just contributing in meetings; he was confidently leading significant project presentations, engaging clients with newfound assurance. This wasn't because he was pushed relentlessly or criticized for his shortcomings. It was because he was understood, supported, and gently guided towards his own latent potential.

That experience crystallized a profound realization for me: True performance enhancement is rarely about applying more pressure or demanding people push harder. More often, it's about identifying and carefully removing the hidden barriers – be they fear, lack of confidence, or skill gaps – and systematically building belief, both in themselves and in their supportive environment.

The Manager's True Calling: From Evaluator to Enabler

At the very core of human-centered performance management lies a simple, yet profoundly transformative truth: your team doesn't need another judge standing ready with a gavel. They are yearning for a partner, a guide, a champion.

Your role, as a manager, transcends the mere act of assessment. Your highest calling is to enable. Yes, you must help people see clearly where they stand, offering honest and constructive feedback. But your responsibility doesn't end there. You must also help them envision where they can go, illuminating the pathways to their potential. You must provide unwavering clarity on expectations, but also offer the right kind of challenge that sparks growth. You must deliver feedback with courage and candor, but always, always, show unwavering faith in their capacity to learn, adapt, and succeed.

When individuals feel not just evaluated, but genuinely supported and appropriately stretched, they don't just strive to meet targets; they begin to actively grow. And when your people grow, the organization, inevitably and wonderfully, grows with them.

Humanizing Performance: Beyond the Metrics to the Heartbeat

Ultimately, managing performance effectively is not about meticulously ticking boxes on a checklist, assigning cold numerical grades, or embarking on a fault-finding mission. It's, at its heart, about the courageous and consistent cultivation of clarity, the unwavering establishment of trust, and the deep fostering of genuine commitment.

It's about daring to have the honest, sometimes difficult, conversations that empower rather than diminish, that build bridges rather than walls. It's about learning to see the people you lead not just through the narrow lens of their immediate output, but through the expansive, hopeful lens of their ongoing growth and their boundless potential.

If you genuinely desire performance to thrive, to become a vibrant and sustainable force within your team and organization, don't begin with pressure. Begin with partnership. As a true partner, commit to tracking the things that truly matter – the progress, the effort, the learning, the collaboration. As James Clear so wisely articulated in his book Atomic Habits, "Track what matters. What gets measured gets improved." Let us ensure we are measuring and improving the human elements that drive lasting success.

> *"Performance Management is a holistic management discipline which needs to connect many relevant dots to involve development, enablement, and enhancement." – Pearl Zhu*

CHAPTER 10

Building High-Trust, High-Performance Teams

"A team is not a group of people who work together. A team is a group of people who trust each other." – Simon Sinek

The Foundation of Every Great Team

Imagine the most impressive structures – towering skyscrapers, intricate bridges. What you see is the marvel of engineering, the gleaming façade. What you don't see is the deep, meticulously laid foundation, the hidden framework that bears the load and allows the structure to reach its potential. In the world of human endeavor, trust is that unseen architecture. Behind every groundbreaking project, every seamless delivery, and every truly exceptional team lies not just a collection of skilled individuals, but a network of people bound by profound, mutual trust.

Trust is the vital current that transforms a group of individuals merely coexisting in a workspace into a cohesive, dynamic team. It's the difference between hesitant cooperation and enthusiastic collaboration. Without it, communication becomes guarded, filtered through layers of caution and self-preservation. Ideas wither before they are spoken, risks are avoided, and collaboration devolves into a series of sterile transactions. Potential lies dormant, choked by suspicion or indifference.

But cultivate trust, and the dynamic shifts entirely. Vulnerability becomes possible, even encouraged. Ideas flow freely, challenged constructively, and built upon collectively. Help is offered proactively, not tracked on a mental ledger. Mistakes are seen not as indictments but as data points for learning and growth. This fertile ground is not cultivated through forced fun or superficial team-building exercises alone. It grows organically, nurtured daily through unwavering consistency, genuine vulnerability, demonstrable fairness, and authentic care woven into the fabric of every interaction.

Sensing the Difference: The Atmosphere of Trust

You can almost feel the atmospheric pressure change when you walk into a high-trust environment versus one simply going through the motions. In teams where trust is the bedrock, meetings crackle with energy – not nervous tension, but the buzz of engaged minds. People speak candidly, offering dissenting opinions without fear of retribution. Laughter is common. Feedback, even when critical, is delivered with respect and received with openness, viewed as a gift aimed at collective improvement. Mistakes aren't hidden or deflected; they are acknowledged openly, dissected for lessons, and integrated into future efforts.

The air is clear of the smog of office politics. There is no undercurrent of gossip, no need to decipher hidden meanings or second-guess colleagues' motives. People operate with the confident assumption of positive intent. They feel intrinsically valued, knowing their contributions are recognized and that setbacks won't be used against them. This environment fosters a powerful dynamic: individuals push each other towards excellence, not out of competitive rivalry, but from a shared desire to elevate the entire team.

This is not an accidental state of grace. It's the deliberate result of leadership that prioritizes psychological safety over rigid control, human connection over bureaucratic process, and learning over the illusion of perfection.

A Story of Unexpected Alchemy

Let me share a moment that crystallized this for me. It was late 2017. I was handed a project that, on paper, looked like a professional nightmare. It was deeply troubled, riddled with legacy issues, and significantly behind schedule. To compound the challenge, the team assigned to salvage it consisted almost entirely of bright-eyed, but utterly inexperienced, recent college graduates. My initial reaction? A knot of anxiety in my stomach. This felt less like a project and more like a guaranteed source of sleepless nights – a perfect recipe for disaster. Any seasoned manager would feel the same pressure, the weight of impending failure.

But as I walked into the workspace on that first day, a different thought surfaced. These young graduates were looking, consciously or not, for cues. If I projected doubt or anxiety, how could they possibly muster the confidence we desperately needed? How could we, as a unit, face this behemoth if our leader was already bracing for impact? In that moment, I made a conscious choice. I mentally shed the "Manager" title, the invisible barrier of hierarchy. I decided to approach them not from a position of authority, but as a fellow traveler on a challenging journey, albeit one with a bit more experience navigating the terrain.

The effect was almost instantaneous, like flipping a switch. By sharing my own initial concerns (phrased as challenges we'd tackle together), by asking for their initial impressions and ideas before offering mine, by simply sitting with them rather than apart, a fragile bridge of trust began to form. It wasn't magic, but it felt close. It was the simple act of being human, vulnerable, and present. I sensed this nascent trust was our most valuable asset, the key to turning this situation around. But it needed reinforcement, a stronger foundation.

We dove into the work, the days inevitably stretching into long evenings. The pressure was immense. Yet, something remarkable happened. Whenever fatigue started to set in, whenever the frustration mounted,

I'd suggest a quick break – not a formal meeting, just a walk to the pantry for coffee or tea. We made an unspoken pact: no work talk during these brief respites. We talked about weekend plans, silly memes, hobbies, the challenges of adjusting to corporate life. We connected as people. They saw I wasn't just a taskmaster demanding hours; I cared about their well-being. They never once questioned my intentions when I encouraged these pauses; the trust was implicit. Because of this bond, the long hours did not feel like drudgery. The work pressure was still there, but it was counterbalanced by a burgeoning camaraderie, a shared sense of purpose, and surprisingly, enjoyment. We weren't just colleagues; we were a unit, facing the fire together.

The ultimate test came during a critical phase requiring an almost unbelievable push – over 50 consecutive hours in the office to meet a non-negotiable deadline. Internally, I harbored doubts. Could we actually, do it? Could anyone sustain that? But before I could even fully articulate a plan, this group of "inexperienced" graduates preempted me. They came together and assured me, with unwavering conviction, "We've got this. We're in this together. We'll see it through." And they did. They supported each other, kept spirits high, and delivered with incredible focus. The entire senior management was astounded, praising the resilience and performance of this "high-performing team" that simply refused to accept defeat.

Years later, most of us have moved on to different teams, even different organizations. But the connection remains. We still check in. When they face a career crossroad or need advice, they reach out without hesitation. That initial investment in trust, built on vulnerability and genuine connection, paid dividends far beyond a single project. It forged lasting relationships.

Building Trust: The Daily Deposits and Withdrawals

Think of trust like a shared bank account. It doesn't materialize overnight with a large, one-time deposit. It grows incrementally, through consistent, positive actions – the small "deposits" made daily. Following through on a commitment, however minor. Owning a mistake openly and honestly, without excuses. Listening intently when someone speaks, putting away distractions. Giving credit generously and publicly where it's due. Defending a team member's reputation in their absence. Each of these actions adds to the balance.

Conversely, trust is fragile. It can be depleted rapidly through "withdrawals." Inconsistent behavior – saying one thing and doing another. Broken promises, even small ones. Showing favoritism or bias. Gossiping or speaking negatively about team members behind their backs. Micromanaging, signaling a lack of faith. These actions, sometimes seemingly insignificant in isolation, can quickly drain the account, eroding the foundation painstakingly built.

Building and maintaining this trust is not accidental; it demands intentional, mindful leadership. It's not about projecting an image of flawless perfection. Paradoxically, it's often the leader's willingness to be imperfect – to admit uncertainty, to acknowledge errors, to show their own humanity – that builds the deepest trust. You earn trust not by wielding control, but by consistently demonstrating credibility (competence and integrity), fairness (impartiality and equity), and presence (being available, attentive, and genuinely invested).

This theoretical framework of trust as an intentionally cultivated account found vivid, practical expression in a leader I had the distinct privilege of working with: Mr. Venkatesh S, then the Head of Business Development at Reliance Life Sciences. He was, in every sense, a brand ambassador for the art of trust-building. The longevity of his team, with members who remained fiercely loyal for years, was a powerful testament to the deep reserves of trust he had meticulously 'deposited.'

Mr. Venkatesh embodied the principle that trust allows for robust, direct communication. He was known for his straightforward, even strict, demeanor and his unwavering commitment to giving unvarnished feedback. In a different context, such candor might have been perceived as a 'withdrawal,' yet within the high-trust environment he fostered, these interactions were rarely taken negatively. I, too, experienced his directness on a couple of occasions; he never sugar-coated his words when delivering feedback aimed at growth.

But the true 'magic,' as you aptly put it, lay in his extraordinary ability to balance this rigor with profound humanity and 'presence.' He demonstrated that strong leadership is not about tiptoeing around issues but about building a foundation where even challenging conversations are received as acts of genuine investment in an individual's development. It was this consistent demonstration of 'credibility' – both in his competence and his unwavering integrity – and 'fairness' that filled the trust account to overflowing. So, even if he addressed a genuine issue with forceful passion, he possessed the remarkable capacity to follow it with a gesture of equally genuine connection and support, perhaps a heartfelt word or, as you experienced, a reassuring hug in the very next moment. This wasn't a display of inconsistency; rather, it was the mark of a leader who was wholly present, deeply invested, and secure enough in the established trust to be both demanding and deeply caring. It's this blend of exacting standards and palpable humanity that made him such a great leader, fostering an environment where his people felt both challenged and cherished. Though my own aspirations eventually led me to a different path, Mr. Venkatesh S remains an indelible figure in my professional journey, a benchmark for the kind of leader who truly understands that trust is the bedrock of exceptional teamwork and loyalty.

Communication: The Oxygen of Trust

If trust is the foundation, then communication is the oxygen that keeps the team alive and thriving. Clear, honest, timely, and respectful communication is the lifeblood. But effective communication transcends the mere exchange of words; it encompasses intent, tone, non-verbal cues, and crucially, the willingness to listen more than you speak.

A leader who fosters trust communicates expectations with unambiguous clarity, ensuring everyone understands the 'what' and the 'why'. They provide feedback regularly – both positive and constructive – with the clear intention of helping individuals and the team grow. They ask powerful questions, questions that invite diverse perspectives and signal that every voice matters. They resist the urge to dominate conversations; instead, they practice deep, active listening – seeking to understand before seeking to be understood. And critically, when they don't have the answers, they admit it. This vulnerability builds far more credibility than feigned omniscience.

Teams don't typically fracture because of difficult conversations or direct feedback delivered respectfully. Trust erodes in the vacuum created by ambiguity, mixed messages, avoidance of crucial topics, or sheer indifference. It's not the presence of challenging discussions that harms a team; it's the absence of open, honest communication that allows misunderstandings to fester and resentment to take root. I've witnessed promising teams crumble simply because critical information failed to flow effectively – either senior leadership directives were diluted or distorted on their way down, or vital ground-level concerns and feedback never made it back up. Bridging these communication gaps is fundamental to maintaining trust.

Alignment: Rowing in the Same Direction

High performance is not just about individual speed or effort; it's about collective velocity towards a shared goal. This requires alignment. Alignment means every single team member understands the overarching mission, their specific role in achieving it, how their work interconnects with others, and the agreed-upon priorities. It ensures clarity on objectives and fosters an environment of mutual support.

Without alignment, teams work at cross-purposes. Individuals might achieve personal wins that don't contribute to the collective goal, or worse, hinder it. Effort is duplicated, deadlines are missed due to unforeseen dependencies, and frustration leads to finger-pointing and territorialism ("That is not my job!"). Energy is wasted on internal friction instead of external progress.

A truly high-performing team operates like a championship rowing crew. Each member is skilled, powerful, and essential. But it's their perfect synchronization, their shared understanding of the rhythm and goal, that propels the boat forward with speed and grace. Each stroke is aligned, contributing to the collective momentum.

Navigating Conflict: Strengthening, Not Shattering, Trust

Disagreement and conflict are inevitable in any group of passionate, intelligent individuals. In fact, a complete absence of conflict can be a red flag, suggesting apathy or fear. Healthy conflict – the vigorous debate of ideas, the challenging of assumptions, the surfacing of blind spots – is often the crucible where the best decisions are forged.

The crucial distinction lies in how conflict is handled. In high-trust teams, conflict remains focused on the issue, not the person. Ideas are debated passionately, but intentions are not attacked. Disagreement occurs without disrespect. People can challenge each other directly, even fiercely, yet maintain underlying rapport because the trust foundation is solid. They operate under the assumption that everyone shares the same ultimate goal: the team's success.

As a leader, your role is paramount in modeling and nurturing healthy conflict resolution. Encourage team members to voice concerns early and directly, rather than letting them fester. When disagreements escalate, facilitate discussion with impartiality and a focus on shared interests. Establish clear norms that prohibit personal attacks, sarcasm, passive aggression, or pulling rank.

Crucially, don't shy away from underlying tensions. If you sense unspoken friction, address it proactively. Teams that habitually avoid conflict often build up a dangerous reservoir of resentment, and resentment is a slow-acting poison that inevitably corrodes trust.

I recall countless instances where team members, frustrated with their direct manager, would bypass them and come straight to me. My default response wasn't to simply delegate it back down. More often than not, I'd bring the individuals and their manager together for a facilitated conversation. My philosophy has always been that even minor conflicts require attention to prevent them from escalating and leaving residual bitterness. It's my responsibility to ensure harmony and clear the air.

One particularly vivid memory involves two senior managers from my team erupting into a full-blown argument during a high-stakes meeting. Voices were raised, accusations flew – it was purely work-related, driven by intense pressure, but it spiraled quickly. Within minutes, one had fired off an email to HR, lodging a formal complaint. The situation felt explosive. Just as I was contemplating the messy path forward, my phone rang. It was my own leader, Mr. Abhishek Garg. He listened patiently as I described the chaos, then, in his characteristically calm manner, offered just three words: "Sort it out." That simple, trusting mandate cut through my paralysis. It was a vote of confidence, empowering me to handle it. I immediately called both managers into a meeting. I did not focus on blame. Instead, I asked them point-blank: did they truly want to escalate this, involving HR and potentially damaging their working relationship, or could we acknowledge that their intense arguments stemmed from a shared, positive intention – ensuring the project's success? I reminded them of their mutual goal. The tension diffused almost instantly. They recognized the shared objective beneath the surface conflict, agreed to retract the complaint, and found a way to move forward collaboratively. Addressing the conflict head-on, grounded in trust and shared purpose, prevented lasting damage.

Recognition and Inclusion

People have an innate need not just to contribute, but to be seen, heard, and valued for their contributions. In high-performing, high-trust teams, recognition is not an afterthought or a formal HR process; it's woven into the daily culture. Inclusion is not about ticking boxes; it's about intentionally creating an environment where everyone feels they belong and their unique perspective is sought after.

Simple acts resonate deeply: a specific, timely note of appreciation for extra effort; publicly acknowledging someone's contribution in a team meeting; celebrating milestones and progress, not just final victories; taking the time to ask someone for their opinion, especially if they tend to be quieter. Inclusion means more than just inviting diverse individuals onto the team; it means actively cultivating an atmosphere where diverse viewpoints are welcomed, explored, and integrated.

Trust flourishes when individuals feel a genuine sense of belonging, when they believe their presence matters and their contributions make a tangible difference to the collective success.

Accountability with Compassion

In some organizational cultures, "accountability" is a loaded term, often synonymous with finding someone to blame when things go wrong. This breeds fear, encourages hiding mistakes, and stifles innovation. In truly great teams, accountability is understood differently: it's a mutual commitment to owning actions, learning from outcomes, and supporting each other in course correction.

When mistakes happen or goals are missed (and they inevitably will), the focus in a high-trust team is not on assigning blame, but on understanding the root cause. What happened? Why did it happen? What can we learn from this? How can we prevent it from happening again? This collective ownership is only possible in an environment where mistakes are treated as valuable feedback and opportunities for growth, not as punishable offenses.

The leader's response sets the tone. If mistakes are met with harsh criticism or punitive measures, the team will quickly learn to conceal problems, deflect responsibility, and avoid taking necessary risks. Conversely, if leaders approach setbacks with curiosity, empathy, and a focus on collaborative problem-solving, they cultivate a culture of psychological safety where individuals feel empowered to take ownership and be truly accountable. Throughout my career, I've consciously avoided punitive actions unless faced with undeniable compliance breaches or integrity violations. Fostering accountability thrives in an atmosphere of support and learning, not fear.

Bridging the Distance: Trust in the Distributed World

In today's landscape of hybrid and fully remote teams, the intentional cultivation of trust becomes even more critical, and arguably, more challenging. The absence of spontaneous hallway conversations, shared coffee breaks, and easily readable in-person body language increases the potential for misunderstandings, assumptions, and feelings of isolation.

Therefore, leaders of distributed teams must be hyper-vigilant and deliberate in their trust-building efforts. This means leaning heavily on transparency – sharing information proactively and widely. It requires heightened responsiveness – acknowledging communications promptly, even if a detailed response needs more time. Empathy becomes paramount – consciously checking in not just on work progress, but on individual well-being, acknowledging the unique challenges of remote work. Communication needs to be more frequent, more explicit, and utilize multiple channels. Virtual team-building needs to be authentic and focus on connection, not just forced fun.

In a world where physical proximity is absent, trust is built and maintained through unwavering consistency, clear communication, demonstrated care, and intentional efforts to bridge the virtual distance.

A Personal Reflection: The Team That Defied the Odds

A few years back, I found myself leading a newly formed project team that was a microcosm of modern challenges: geographically dispersed across multiple cities, culturally diverse, operating under relentless deadline pressure, and tackling a very demanding client. By all conventional metrics, we were set up for struggle, and indeed, the initial days were fraught with missteps and friction. Communication lagged, misunderstandings arose, and the differences of opinions created hurdles. We stumbled.

Yet, within a few months, something shifted dramatically. Not only did we stabilize, but we began to excel, ultimately exceeding every performance target set for us. How? The answer wasn't a new tool or process. It was simpler and more profound: we built genuine trust across the distances.

How did we do it? We were rigorously honest – admitting when we were stuck, confused, or overwhelmed. We established clear communication protocols but also made space for informal virtual "water cooler" chats. We actively learned about each other's styles. We covered for each other without keeping score, driven by a sense of shared responsibility. We provided feedback openly and constructively, always assuming positive intent. And crucially, even amidst the intense pressure, we found ways to inject humor and humanity into our virtual interactions – sharing jokes, celebrating small wins publicly, acknowledging personal milestones.

That experience powerfully reinforced a core belief: technology and processes are enablers, but they don't build trust. People do. Through intentional acts of vulnerability, empathy, reliability, and connection.

And when that trust exists, even the most daunting challenges – distance, diversity, pressure – become surmountable obstacles that a united team can rise above, together.

Trust Is the Culture; Performance Is the Outcome

Ultimately, the quest for high performance begins not with demands and pressure, but with fostering an environment where people feel psychologically safe, deeply respected, genuinely included, and meaningfully empowered.

Don't lead by instilling fear; lead by providing clarity of purpose and expectation. Don't manage through tight control; manage with compassion and genuine care for your people's well-being. Don't fixate solely on the what – the deliverables and metrics; pay equal attention to the how – the emotional and psychological experience of the team members as they strive to deliver. As Robert Iger aptly stated in The Ride of a Lifetime, "Empathy is a prerequisite to leadership... A culture of respect and candor drives excellence."

Because sustainable, exceptional performance is not merely a product of optimized systems or efficient processes. It's the natural, emergent outcome of a culture steeped in psychological safety, united by a shared purpose, and built upon the bedrock of real, human trust.

"Without trust we don't truly collaborate; we merely coordinate or, at best, cooperate. It's trust that transforms a group of people into a team." – Stephen Covey

CHAPTER 11

Coaching, Feedback, and Growth Conversations

"The greatest gift we can give is helping someone see the strength they already have." – Ben Killoy

The Shift from Supervision to Coaching

Picture the traditional landscape of management: a towering figure, the supervisor, perched atop a hierarchy. Their role? To dictate, to monitor, to correct, to ensure tasks were executed with precision, often within tightly defined parameters. The employee, in this paradigm, was the diligent implementer, the follower of directives. This model, born of an industrial age, served its purpose for a time. But the tectonic plates of our work environments have shifted. The ground beneath us is no longer static; it's a fluid, ever-evolving terrain of collaboration, innovation, and rapid change.

In this vibrant, new ecosystem, the old crown of "supervisor" feels heavy, anachronistic. Modern leadership whispers a different calling, a profound transformation: from the watchful eye of the supervisor to the guiding hand of the coach. This is not merely a change in job title; it's a fundamental reimagining of a leader's purpose.

Coaching, in its truest sense, is not about hovering with a red pen, poised to strike at every deviation from your prescribed path. It's a far more profound, more human endeavor. It's about igniting the spark of self-discovery within your team members. It's about fostering an environment where reflection is not a luxury but a routine, where individuals are empowered to unearth their own solutions, to innovate, and to own their journey. The core belief here is revolutionary for some: people are inherently resourceful, brimming with latent capabilities. Your privilege as a leader is to be the catalyst, the gentle force that helps them uncork that wellspring of potential.

This journey into coaching leadership begins not with a playbook of directives, but with two deeply human qualities: genuine curiosity and authentic care. It's rooted in the understanding that sustainable growth, the kind that truly transforms individuals and teams, rarely sprouts from being constantly told what to do. Instead, it blossoms when people are invited into a richer dialogue – a dialogue that encourages them to think with greater depth, to question assumptions, and to act with heightened intention and ownership.

The Essence of the Coach-Manager: Strength in Nurturing

To the uninitiated, this empathetic, question-led approach might seem... soft. Some might misinterpret it as a leader lacking decisiveness, perhaps even someone passive, adrift in a sea of gentle suggestions. But let's dispel that myth with vigor. Being a coach-manager is the antithesis of passivity. It's an active, dynamic, and courageous form of leadership.

It demands acute emotional intelligence: the wisdom to discern when to intervene with guidance, when to step back and pose a thought-provoking question instead of spoon-feeding an answer, and precisely when to nudge someone beyond the familiar confines of their comfort zone, towards that fertile ground where real growth occurs.

A manager who embodies the coaching spirit sees their team not as a collection of interchangeable cogs in a machine, but as a vibrant tapestry of individuals, each on a unique developmental trajectory. They become adept at recognizing patterns – in behavior, in thought processes, in successes, and in setbacks. They don't just point out flaws;

they facilitate reflection. They guide their people towards clarity, not by delivering sermons from a pedestal, but by engaging in meaningful, often courageous, conversations.

Consider this: offering unsolicited advice is often the path of least resistance. It's quick, it makes us feel knowledgeable. But to craft the right question – the one that pierces through surface-level thinking and sparks genuine introspection – and then to wait, with unwavering patience and complete presence, for another human being to wrestle with it and arrive at their own profound insight? That is an art. That is the harder, more rewarding path. That is the mark of a true coach-manager.

Feedback: The Cornerstone of Growth – If Crafted with Care

Among the myriad responsibilities of a people manager, delivering feedback stands as one of the most pivotal, yet often, most awkwardly handled. Many leaders, candidly, would rather walk over hot coals. Some dance around the subject with such elaborate euphemisms that the core message dissolves into a sugary fog. Others, fearing conflict or discomfort, avoid it altogether, allowing small issues to fester and grow. Then there are those who deliver it with the subtlety of a sledgehammer, leaving a trail of bruised egos and damaged trust.

But what if we re-framed feedback? At its most profound, feedback is not a critique aimed at diminishing someone. It's, in fact, a profound act of respect and investment. It's a declaration that says, "I am invested enough in your journey, in your potential, to share an observation that might be outside your current field of vision. I care enough to help you grow."

The most transformative feedback possesses distinct characteristics: it's timely, delivered close enough to the event or behavior in question that it remains relevant. It's laser-specific, focusing on concrete actions and observable behaviors, not on vague personality traits or, worse, assumptions about intent. "You seem disengaged" is an accusation. "I noticed during the last three team meetings that you did not contribute to the brainstorming sessions, and your weekly reports have been submitted past the deadline. I'm wondering what might be contributing to this, and how I can support you" – this is an invitation to a constructive dialogue.

Let's delve into a real-world illustration. If you remember, I had spoken about Dr. Prasad Apsangikar, in Chapter 6. He was known for his calm demeanor and unwavering support for his team. Yet, when feedback was necessary, it was delivered with a potent blend of clarity and empathy, always punctually. There was no shouting, no belittling, but also no tiptoeing around the issue. His directness was empowering because it was always coupled with a genuine desire to see the person succeed.

One of his team members, let's call him Siddhant, was bright but struggling. His contributions were inconsistent, and he wasn't being taken seriously by peers or stakeholders. Deadlines were missed, and key responsibilities were fumbled. Many managers, faced with this, might have resorted to a stern lecture, a list of failings. Dr. Prasad chose a different path. He invited Siddhant for a conversation, not an interrogation. He began by expressing his observations neutrally and then asked open-ended questions: "Sid, I've noticed a few challenges with your deliverables recently, and I sense there might be something more going on. Can you share what your experience has been like lately? Have you been facing any problem which you would like to discuss in detail with me?"

It took time, and a safe space, for Siddhant to open up. It turned out there wasn't a single, glaring reason for his underperformance, but rather a confluence of minor uncertainties and a dip in confidence. Dr. Prasad listened intently. Then, instead of simply criticizing, he said, "Sid, I understand things have been challenging. Since we haven't pinpointed a specific external blocker, I believe a structured developmental action plan would be beneficial. This is not a punitive measure; quite the opposite. I want to personally work with you on this, to provide the support and guidance you need to get back on track and excel in your role. My goal is to see you succeed." The outcome? Over the ensuing months, with targeted coaching and regular check-ins from Dr. Prasad, Siddhant underwent a remarkable transformation, not just meeting but exceeding expectations.

This is the essence of developmental feedback. It's not a weapon to be wielded during annual performance reviews. It's a continuous conversation, a thread woven into the fabric of daily interactions. When delivered with empathy, clarity, and a genuine commitment to development, feedback doesn't fracture relationships; it forges stronger, more resilient bonds.

The Unspoken Dialogue

A common oversight in the leadership narrative is the perception of feedback as a one-way transmission: from manager to employee. But this misses a critical dimension. The most vibrant, high-trust teams are those where feedback flows freely in all directions, including upwards.

Imagine a team where individuals feel genuinely safe to offer constructive insights to their manager, knowing it will be received with humility and openness, not defensiveness or retribution. In such an environment, trust doesn't just exist; it flourishes. Conversely, when team members bite their tongues, when they fear speaking truth to power, small misalignments can widen into gaping chasms, and the crucial "ground truth" of team morale and operational realities becomes obscured.

Proactive leaders don't wait for the formal, often sanitized, 360-degree feedback cycle mandated by HR. They actively cultivate channels for receiving feedback. They make it a norm. This could be through posing direct questions in one-on-ones: "What's one thing I could start doing, stop doing, or continue doing that would better support you and the team?" or "If you were in my shoes, what's one change you'd make to improve our collective effectiveness?"

And when this feedback arrives – sometimes unvarnished, sometimes tentative – the leader's response is paramount. The instinct might be to explain, to justify. Resist it. Listen. Truly listen. Absorb it. Express gratitude for the courage and candor it took to share. Then, take time to reflect on it honestly and, where appropriate, take visible action. This act of receiving feedback gracefully, and acting upon it, is a powerful signal. It tells the team: "Your voice matters. I am also a work in progress. We are in this together." Don't solely rely on survey data, which can often present a filtered or delayed picture. Keep your ear to the ground, be attuned to the subtle cues, the unsaid words, the emotional temperature of your team. A leader who humbly accepts and acts on feedback builds a fortress of psychological safety.

Beyond the Annual Ritual: Weaving Growth into Daily Conversations

We've touched upon the limitations of confining growth discussions to the once-a-year appraisal in Chapter 9. True developmental dialogues are not checkboxes on a calendar; they are vibrant, ongoing explorations. They delve into an individual's aspirations – not just for the next promotion, but for the skills they yearn to cultivate, the experiences they wish to gain. They shine a light on existing strengths, helping individuals leverage them more effectively, and they gently explore blind spots, not as failings, but as opportunities for deeper self-awareness and development.

These conversations are propelled by curiosity: "Looking ahead this year, where do you envision your most significant growth?" or "What new skills or knowledge areas are you passionate about developing, and how can we weave that into your current role or future projects?" The intent transcends mere performance assessment; it's about nurturing ambition, identifying and providing stretch assignments that push boundaries, and keeping the flame of learning perpetually alive.

It's a startling truth that many employees harbor unspoken growth goals simply because no one ever thought to ask. When you, as a leader, deliberately carve out space for these conversations, you send an unequivocal message: "Your personal and professional evolution is a priority here. Your journey matters to me, and to this organization."

Suddenly, you begin to see your team members not as static units of productivity, but as dynamic, evolving professionals, each navigating a unique and fascinating path. Your role shifts from taskmaster to a partner in their development, a co-navigator on their journey of growth.

Guiding Through the Storm

The true mettle of a coach-manager is often tested not in the calm waters of routine success, but in the turbulent seas of struggle. It's when a team member is drowning in the complexities of a challenging project, when their confidence is shattered by an unexpected failure, or when interpersonal friction threatens to derail collaboration – these are the moments when coaching is not just valuable, it's vital.

The instinctual response might be to jump in and rescue, to provide the solution, to take over the reins. But this, while perhaps offering temporary relief, often disempowers in the long run. True coaching in these crucible moments involves a different approach. It's about asking empowering questions: "This is clearly a tough situation. What aspect of it feels most overwhelming for you right now?" or "If we were to look back on this challenge successfully navigated, what would that success look like from your perspective? What's one small step you could take today towards that vision?"

You don't need to be the hero who slays their dragons. Your role is to stand beside them, a steady presence. To illuminate the path with insightful questions, and then, crucially, to trust in their capacity to find their own way forward. Often, the simple act of being deeply heard, of having their struggle validated, and being guided by thoughtful inquiry is the catalyst an individual needs to regroup, regain their footing, and bounce back with renewed resilience and determination.

The Echo of Feedback

One of the most common, and frustrating, pitfalls in leadership is the "feedback-and-flee" syndrome. A manager delivers feedback, perhaps even constructive and well-intentioned, and then... radio silence. The employee is left wondering: Did it land? Was it serious? What am I supposed to do with this now? This creates not just confusion, but often anxiety and a sense of being judged and abandoned.

Feedback should never feel like a drive-by critique. It's the beginning of a dialogue, not the end of one. When you offer insights, especially those that point towards areas for improvement, commit to the follow-through. Schedule a check-in: "I wanted to see how you're feeling about our conversation last week and if you've had a chance to reflect on the feedback." Ask how it landed, if they require additional support, resources, or clarification. And, importantly, be vigilant for and enthusiastically celebrate any improvements or efforts made, no matter how small. Reinforce the positive changes.

When feedback is integrated into a sustained, trusting engagement – a continuous loop of conversation, support, and accountability – it becomes a powerful lever for genuine behavioral shifts and strengthens the psychological safety net that allows individuals to take risks and grow.

The Personal Palette: Tailoring Your Coaching Canvas

Human beings are wonderfully diverse, and so too are their responses to coaching and feedback. A one-size-fits-all approach is destined for mediocrity. Some individuals thrive on direct, unvarnished communication. Others need a softer entry, perhaps with more space to process information privately before discussing it. Some learn best through concrete examples and case studies; others connect more deeply with a narrative, a metaphor, or a story that resonates with their experience.

The astute coach-manager becomes a student of their people. They learn to adapt their style, their timing, their language, based on the unique personality and learning preferences of the individual they are coaching. This is not about playing favorites; it's about maximizing effectiveness. The ultimate goal is for the message to be received, understood, and acted upon in a way that fosters growth. If your tone is off-putting, if your timing is insensitive, or if your words fail to connect, even the most valuable insight can be lost in translation.

So, become an observer. Pay attention to how different team members react. Ask them directly: "What's the most effective way for me to share feedback with you?" or "When you're learning something new, what helps it click for you?" The more attuned your coaching becomes to the individual, the more deeply it will resonate, and the more profound its impact will be.

Seeds Don't Sprout Immediately

There will inevitably be times when your most earnest coaching efforts don't yield immediate, visible results. Progress might be painstakingly slow. Old, ingrained habits may prove stubbornly resistant to change. In these moments, the temptation can be to feel frustrated, to panic, or even to give up on the individual.

Resist that temptation. Coaching is akin to planting seeds. Not all seeds germinate at the same rate, and not all flowers bloom on a predictable schedule. Your role is to continue nurturing the soil. Maintain a supportive and encouraging tone, even when delivering challenging messages. Hold the line on clear expectations of performance and behavior, but offer unwavering belief in their capacity to meet those expectations, coupled with the necessary time and resources.

As Nick Trenton wisely noted in "Stop Overthinking," a key aspect of helping others is to guide them in quieting their own inner critic, that harsh voice that can drown out even the most constructive feedback. People unlock their potential for change when they feel fundamentally safe, genuinely seen, and consistently supported – not when they feel prematurely judged or written off. Patience, in coaching, is not just a virtue; it's a strategic imperative.

Grow With Them, Not Just Ahead of Them

Ultimately, coaching, the art of giving and receiving feedback, and the cultivation of growth conversations are not elective modules in the curriculum of leadership. They are the very heart of it. They are the daily practices that transform managers into true leaders.

You don't need a formal certification hanging on your wall to be an effective coach. What you need is a deep well of care for the people you lead, the discipline to listen with an intent to understand rather than to reply, and the courage to speak your truth with honesty and compassion. Above all, you need an unshakeable belief in the inherent desire of people to learn, to develop, and to contribute meaningfully – and to see your role as walking alongside them on that journey, offering guidance and support, rather than striding far ahead and expecting them to simply keep up.

When your team members know, deep in their bones, that you're profoundly invested in their evolution – not just in their immediate output or efficiency – something magical happens. Trust solidifies. Engagement deepens. Discretionary effort is unlocked. And they not only perform better, but they also choose to stay and grow with you, contributing to a culture of continuous development and shared success.

> *"Great leaders can see the greatness in others when they can't see it themselves and lead them to their highest potential they don't even know." – Roy T. Bennett*

Part IV

Tough Moments and Real Leadership

CHAPTER 12

Navigating Difficult Conversations and Conflicts

"Leaders do not avoid, repress, or deny conflict, but rather see it as an opportunity." – Warren G Bennis

The quote by Bennis serves not just as an opening line, but as a guiding principle for effective leadership in complex environments. It challenges the conventional, often uncomfortable, view of conflict and invites us to see beyond the initial discomfort towards the potential for growth and strengthening. It sets the stage for understanding why embracing, rather than fearing, conflict is a hallmark of impactful leadership.

The Unavoidable Landscape of Workplace Conflict

In the dynamic ecosystem of any organization, conflict is not a deviation from the norm; it's an inherent feature of human interaction. Placing diverse individuals – with varying backgrounds, experiences, communication styles, values, and aspirations – into a shared space, often under pressure, with competing priorities and deadlines, naturally breeds friction. Difference of opinion is merely the surface; beneath lie potential misunderstandings, unmet expectations, clashes over resources, and the subtle (or not so subtle) rubbing of personalities.

To pretend conflict doesn't exist, or worse, to actively suppress it, is like ignoring a chronic illness. It doesn't disappear. Instead, it metastasizes, spreading silently through the organization's bloodstream. Trust, the very foundation of effective teamwork, erodes like sand through fingers. Motivation wanes as unresolved issues create simmering resentment. Collaboration breaks down, replaced by guarded interactions and siloed thinking. What started as a minor disagreement can calcify into a permanent divide, hindering productivity and poisoning the organizational culture.

As a people manager, your mandate is not to sterilize the environment of all disagreement – an impossible and undesirable feat, as disagreement, handled well, can spur innovation. Your true power lies in your ability to skillfully, calmly, and constructively navigate these turbulent waters. As we touched upon the importance of addressing issues rather than letting them fester in Chapter 10, specifically when discussing maintaining team dynamics and communication flows, this chapter dedicates itself entirely to the 'how' and 'why' of mastering this crucial, and often challenging, leadership skill. It moves beyond the recognition of the need to address issues and into the practical application of doing so effectively.

Unpacking the Deep-Seated Fear of Tough Talks

Why do so many of us, managers included, recoil at the prospect of a difficult conversation? The roots of this aversion run deep, tapping into fundamental human fears:

- Fear of Harming Relationships: We are social creatures, and the potential for damaging rapport, creating animosity, or being disliked is genuinely unsettling.
- Fear of Escalation: What if the conversation spins out of control? What if the other person gets angry, cries, or reacts in a way we feel unprepared to handle? The unknown is often scarier than the known, even if the known is current discomfort.
- Fear of Being Misunderstood: We worry our intentions will be misinterpreted, that we will come across as unfair, overly critical, or lacking empathy.

- Fear of Our Own Emotions: Difficult conversations can trigger our own anxieties, frustrations, or defensiveness. We may fear losing composure or saying something we regret.
- Fear of Inadequacy: Many managers simply haven't been trained in conflict resolution. They lack a clear framework or practical tools, leading to a feeling of being fundamentally unprepared.

This fear is natural, understandable, even valid up to a point. However, succumbing to it renders leadership incomplete. Leadership is not about maintaining superficial calm; it's about having the courage to address underlying tensions for the long-term health of the team and organization. The true measure of a leader's maturity often manifests in their willingness and ability to step into discomfort rather than sidestep it.

Here is a critical reframing: Conflict, in itself, doesn't break trust. Avoiding the conversation, tiptoeing around the issue, allowing problems to fester in silence – that is what fractures trust and respect. Trust is built not on the absence of conflict, but on the confidence that issues will be addressed fairly, openly, and with respect.

Reframing Conflict: An Opportunity for Growth and Clarity

One of the most powerful shifts you can make is in how you perceive conflict. If you view it solely as a confrontation, a battle to be won or lost, you approach it with a defensive or aggressive mindset. If, however, you reframe it as an opportunity, the landscape changes entirely.

Difficult conversations are fertile ground for:

- Clarifying Values and Expectations: Often, conflict arises from mismatched assumptions about roles, responsibilities, or performance standards. A difficult conversation provides a necessary reset.
- Deepening Understanding: Stepping into the tension with curiosity allows you to uncover underlying issues, motivations, and perspectives you might have missed.

- Fostering Innovation: Productive disagreement, where ideas clash respectfully, can lead to better solutions and more creative outcomes than homogenous agreement.
- Building Resilience: Successfully navigating conflict strengthens relationships and builds the team's capacity to handle future challenges.
- Demonstrating Leadership Presence: Your willingness to step into uncomfortable territory with grace and purpose signals strength, fairness, and commitment to your team's well-being.

Every awkward moment, every tense exchange, holds the potential to be a turning point – a moment where a relationship deepens, a chronic issue is resolved, or a new level of understanding is reached. It's not about dominating the conversation or avoiding discomfort; it's about achieving alignment, restoring respect, and clearing the air for productive collaboration.

As Daniel Kahneman illuminates in "Thinking, Fast and Slow," our immediate reaction to conflict often triggers System 1 thinking – fast, intuitive, emotional, and prone to biases like fight or flight. Navigating conflict effectively demands engaging System 2 thinking – slow, deliberate, analytical. This requires a conscious pause. Giving yourself time to prepare, to breathe, to analyze the situation rationally before reacting emotionally is not a luxury; it's essential for a productive outcome.

Preparation: Your Compass in the Storm

Approaching a difficult conversation without adequate preparation is akin to sailing into rough seas blindfolded. Preparation provides focus, reduces anxiety by giving you a roadmap, and significantly increases the likelihood of achieving a positive outcome.

Before you initiate the discussion, engage in a thorough self-briefing:

- Define Your Intent and Desired Outcome: Be crystal clear. What, specifically, do you want to achieve by the end of this conversation? Is it a change in behavior? A clearer understanding? A mutual agreement on next steps? Make it measurable and realistic. Your intent should be constructive – to solve a problem, improve performance, strengthen a relationship – never to punish or blame.

- Identify the Specific Issue/Behavior: General complaints are unhelpful. Focus on concrete, observable behavior or a specific situation. Instead of "You're negative," think: "During the team meeting yesterday, when X was discussed, I noticed comments that seemed to undermine the proposed solution."
- Gather Your Facts: Base your concerns on observable data, specific examples, and facts, not assumptions or hearsay. What happened? When did it happen? What was the impact? The more specific you can be, the harder it's for the other person to dispute the premise of the conversation. Think "Situation-Behavior-Impact" (SBI) framework: In situation X, you did behavior Y, which had impact Z.
- Anticipate the Other Person's Perspective and Reaction: Step into their shoes. How might they see this situation? What might be their motivations or fears? What potential defenses or explanations might they offer? Mentally preparing for potential reactions (defensiveness, denial, anger, tears) allows you to respond with more composure and empathy.
- Plan Your Opening: The first few sentences are critical. Plan how you'll invite them into the conversation in a non-threatening way.
- Check Your Emotional State: Are you feeling angry, frustrated, anxious? If your emotions are running high, take time to manage them before the conversation. This doesn't mean suppressing them, but acknowledging them and ensuring they don't hijack the discussion. Deep breaths, a short walk, or talking it through with a trusted peer (while maintaining confidentiality) can help you achieve a state of calm focus.

This focus on preparation and emotional poise was something I particularly learned from observing leaders like Dr. Swapnil Babasaheb Khot. He consistently advocates for the preparatory phase, emphasizing that thorough preparation significantly increases the chances of navigating challenges successfully. I vividly recall a situation in a meeting where emotions were running high, and a participant was visibly distressed and speaking impulsively. Dr. Khot calmly but firmly interrupted, not to silence her feelings, but to gently suggest she take a moment, compose herself, and rejoin the discussion when she felt more centered and able to articulate her points with clarity. His message was clear: emotions are valid and part of the human experience, but in a professional context, they are most impactful when channeled constructively and supported by clear rationale and facts. You do not have to be emotionless, but you must be in control of how you express and act upon your emotions. This principle of pausing to allow for slow, deliberate thinking, and ensuring emotional expression is coupled with factual basis, is a powerful cornerstone of effective preparation for any difficult interaction.

Preparation is not about scripting every line or predicting every turn; it's about establishing a clear purpose, grounding yourself in facts, and approaching the interaction with intentionality and emotional regulation. It's, indeed, more than half the battle won before the first word is spoken.

The Significance of Timing and Setting

The environment in which a difficult conversation takes place can profoundly influence its outcome. A poorly chosen time or location can instantly erect barriers and trigger defensiveness.

Avoid Public or Semi-Public Spaces: Hallways, open-plan offices, crowded break rooms, or even correcting someone in front of their team are absolute no-gos. Public feedback or correction is humiliating and breeds resentment.

Ensure Sufficient Time: Difficult conversations cannot be squeezed into the five minutes before another meeting. They require focused attention without the pressure of the clock ticking down. Estimate the time needed and book a meeting room or schedule a dedicated call.

Choose a Neutral and Private Setting: A private office, a neutral meeting room, or a secure virtual call where distractions are minimized and confidentiality is assured are ideal. This signals that the conversation is important and deserves dedicated, private attention.

Provide Advance Notice (Often): While sometimes immediate feedback is necessary, for planned difficult conversations, giving the person a heads-up allows them to prepare emotionally. A simple, "Hey, can we schedule some time tomorrow to talk about X? I'd like to get your perspective and find a way forward," is far better than blindsiding them with a heavy topic. The goal is sincerity and resolution, not surprise or ambush.

Your choice of setting and timing communicates respect and intent before you even begin speaking. It sets the stage for either a constructive dialogue or a guarded, defensive exchange.

Starting the Conversation: Setting a Collaborative Tone

The opening of a difficult conversation sets the tone and can significantly impact how the rest of it unfolds. Launching directly into criticism or accusations will instantly put the other person on the defensive.

Instead, aim for an opening that is:

- Contextual: Briefly state the reason for the conversation without immediately assigning blame.
- Intent-Based: Clearly articulate your positive intention for the conversation.
- Collaborative: Frame it as a discussion you want to have with them, not something you're doing to them.

- Examples of constructive openings:
- "Thanks for meeting with me. I wanted to talk about [specific situation or project] because I've noticed [specific behavior/outcome], and I'd like to understand your perspective and figure out how we can address it together."
- "I've been thinking about [issue], and it's important to me that we're aligned on this. My goal in talking is to make sure we both understand each other and find a way forward that works."
- "There's something that's been on my mind regarding [topic], and I wanted to discuss it openly with you. My intention is to resolve this so we can work more effectively as a team/together."

Crucially, ground your opening in observation, not accusation. Compare:

Accusation: "You were totally unhelpful in that meeting." (Judgmental, focuses on identity/character)

Observation: "In yesterday's meeting, I noticed you didn't speak up when asked for input on X project, which left the team uncertain about your progress." (Factual, focuses on specific behavior and impact)

This objective approach minimizes defensiveness and invites a more open exchange about the facts of the situation.

The Unparalleled Power of Deep Listening

Once you've initiated the conversation, your most potent tool is your ability to listen – truly listen. Many managers enter difficult conversations with their response already formulated, waiting impatiently for their turn to speak. This is a fundamental error. The other person has their own experience, their own perspective, their own fears and frustrations contributing to the situation.

Create genuine space for them to speak. Ask open-ended questions like:

- "How do you see this situation?"
- "What's been your experience from your perspective?"
- "Can you walk me through what happened from your point of view?"
- "What challenges have you been facing regarding this?"

Then, pause. Lean in. Maintain eye contact. Listen not just to the words, but to the underlying emotions and concerns. Resist the urge to interrupt, to defend yourself, or to formulate your counter-argument while they are still speaking. Practice active listening techniques: nod, use mirroring phrases ("So, if I understand correctly..."), summarize what you've heard ("It sounds like you're feeling frustrated because...").

Often, simply giving someone the floor, making them feel heard and validated, can significantly de-escalate tension and shift the conversation from defensive posturing to collaborative problem-solving. This echoes the power observed when someone is allowed to fully articulate their perspective without interruption – the act of being truly heard can be incredibly disarming and opening. It clears the emotional backlog, allowing for a more rational discussion to follow.

I recall a particular situation with a client who was expressing significant dissatisfaction with the project's progress. Their emails were sharp, and my team felt increasingly defensive, leading to strained interactions where neither side truly absorbed what the other was saying. The communication had deteriorated into a cycle of accusations and justifications. I reached out to the client and scheduled a dedicated call, not to debate or defend, but purely to listen. For the first twenty minutes, perhaps more, I simply allowed them to express all their frustrations, concerns, and the negative impact they felt. I didn't interrupt or try to fix things. I just listened, occasionally nodding or offering a simple "I understand" or "Tell me more."

As they spoke, the initial intensity gradually subsided. The act of being fully heard seemed to release some of the pent-up frustration. Once they had fully aired their perspective, the tone of the conversation shifted. The defensiveness on their end softened, making them more receptive to hearing our perspective and engaging in a constructive dialogue about solutions. What started with high tension ended with a clearer path forward and a noticeable improvement in the client's relationship with the team.

This illustrates the profound magic of listening. It's a powerful, often underutilized, tool. You should ideally apply the same strategy to all your conversations whether it may be with an external stakeholder or internal, whether with a senior person or may be your subordinate. By prioritizing understanding before response, you build trust and create the space needed for genuine resolution.

Listening is not passive; it's an active, empathetic choice that builds bridges where conflict has created divides.

Empathy: The Bridge Across Emotional Divides

Empathy is not about agreeing with someone's perspective or excusing their behavior. It's about the willingness and ability to understand and acknowledge their feelings and the situation from their point of view.

Behind every difficult behavior – be it defensiveness, withdrawal, or frustration – there is usually an underlying human reason: stress, fear (of failure, of judgment, of losing their job), feeling misunderstood, feeling undervalued, feeling overwhelmed. Leading with curiosity rather than judgment helps you uncover these root causes.

Expressing empathy humanizes the interaction. Phrases like:

- "That sounds like a really challenging situation."
- "I can see why you would feel frustrated/upset/concerned about that."

- "It must have been tough dealing with X."
- "Thank you for sharing that; I appreciate you helping me understand your perspective."

These phrases do not equate to agreement. They simply acknowledge the other person's emotional reality. Showing empathy doesn't make you weak; it demonstrates emotional intelligence, courage, and a commitment to treating others with dignity, even when addressing difficult issues. Managers sometimes falter here, believing empathy signals agreement, but it signals understanding and respect – essential components for resolving conflict constructively.

Delivering Feedback: Targeted Towards Growth, Not Blame

Difficult conversations often involve delivering feedback, particularly about performance or behavior that is causing problems. This is where feedback can feel most loaded, as the recipient may already be on edge. How you frame and deliver this feedback is paramount to ensuring it lands constructively rather than crushing the other person's spirit.

Always focus feedback on specific, observable behavior and its impact, never on the person's identity, character, or perceived intentions.

Instead of "You're careless and disorganized." (Attacks identity), say, "I noticed that the report submitted on Tuesday was missing section 3, and this caused confusion for the client during the presentation."

This behavioral focus keeps the conversation objective and actionable. Behavior can be changed; character attacks lead to defensiveness and shame.

Furthermore, balance critique with possibility and partnership. After describing the behavior and its impact, immediately pivot towards solutions and future improvement.

Instead of "This can't happen again." (Demanding, ends negatively), say, "What steps could we put in place to ensure all sections are included in future reports?" or "What support or resources might help you double-check the report before submission going forward?"

This shifts the focus from blame for the past to ownership and growth for the future. You're not just pointing out what went wrong; you're partnering with them to figure out how to make it right next time.

Managing Emotional Escalation

Despite your best efforts, some difficult conversations will involve heightened emotions. The other person might become angry, defensive, withdrawn, or even cry. It's crucial in these moments not to mirror their intensity.

Your role is to remain the calm anchor in the storm. Stay grounded. Speak slowly and calmly. If you feel yourself getting pulled into the emotional vortex, recognize it and take a deliberate pause.

Strategies for managing escalation:

- Stay Calm: Control your breathing. Lower your voice. Maintain open, non-threatening body language.
- Acknowledge the Emotion: Without judgment, you can say, "I can see this is upsetting for you," or "It seems like you're feeling frustrated." This shows you've noticed without necessarily agreeing with the reason for the emotion.
- Take a Break: If emotions become overwhelming for either party, call a temporary halt. "I can see we're both getting heated. Let's take a 15-minute break and reconvene, shall we?" or "Let's pause here and revisit this conversation later today or tomorrow when we've both had a chance to cool down." It's infinitely better to pause and regroup than to say things you regret or let the conversation devolve into an irreparable conflict.

- Set Boundaries (If Necessary): While rare, if the other person's behavior becomes disrespectful or abusive, you must set a boundary. "I understand you're angry, but I cannot continue this conversation if you're yelling/using that language. We can continue when we can speak respectfully."

Remember your goal: repair, rebuild, and realign. Escalation serves none of these purposes. Staying calm and offering a pathway to pause demonstrates strong leadership and a commitment to resolving the issue constructively, even under duress.

Mediating Conflict Between Team Members

Leadership often requires stepping into the role of facilitator when conflict arises between team members. You're no longer a party to the conflict but the steward responsible for guiding others towards resolution. This is a delicate balancing act, much like the scenarios we discussed in Chapter 10 regarding fostering positive team dynamics and intervening when communication breaks down.

Your process as a facilitator might involve:

- Meeting Separately (Initially): Understand each person's perspective individually. Listen deeply to their account of the situation, their feelings, and what they believe the core issue is. This builds trust and gives you a fuller picture.
- Bringing Them Together: Facilitate a joint conversation.
- Setting Ground Rules: Start by establishing expectations for the discussion: respectful listening, no interruptions, focusing on the issue not the person, speaking from 'I' statements (e.g., "I felt X when Y happened") rather than 'You' statements ("You always do Z").
- Guiding the Dialogue: Encourage each person to share their perspective using the ground rules. Ensure equal airtime. Help them articulate their feelings and needs clearly. Reframe

accusations into observations. Guide them towards identifying the root causes of the conflict together.

- Focusing on Solutions: Once the issue is understood, shift the conversation towards finding mutually acceptable solutions. "Given what we've discussed, how can we work together differently going forward?" "What steps can you both agree to take to prevent this from happening again?"

- Maintaining Neutrality: Avoid taking sides or appearing to favor one person's perspective over the other's. Your credibility as a facilitator rests on your perceived fairness and impartiality.

- Knowing When to Escalate: For severe conflicts, issues involving harassment or discrimination, or situations where your mediation is ineffective, do not hesitate to involve HR or a professional mediator. Delaying intervention when you're out of your depth can cause significant harm.

Unresolved team conflict is a toxic agent that degrades morale, productivity, and the overall team dynamic. Addressing it promptly, even if uncomfortable, is a non-negotiable leadership responsibility.

The Crucial Post-Conversation Follow-Through

The difficult conversation itself is often just one step in the resolution process. What happens after the conversation is equally important for ensuring the issue is truly resolved and the relationship is strengthened.

Summarize Agreements: Before ending the conversation, clearly recap any agreed-upon actions, next steps, or commitments from both parties.

Schedule Check-ins: Don't let silence undo the progress. Schedule a follow-up conversation – maybe a week or two later – to see how things are progressing, address any lingering issues, and reinforce positive changes. A brief check-in shows you're committed to the outcome and the person's success.

Monitor Progress (Without Hovering): Observe behavior and outcomes related to the issue you discussed. Acknowledge positive changes when you see them. If the issue resurfaces, be prepared to address it again promptly, perhaps revisiting the strategies discussed.

Rebuild the Relationship: Difficult conversations can strain relationships. Actively work to rebuild trust and rapport through positive interactions, recognition, and continued open communication.

Reflect and Learn: After the conversation (and follow-through), take time to reflect on how it went. What worked well? What could you have done differently? Each difficult conversation is a learning opportunity for you as a leader.

Consistent follow-through demonstrates that the conversation was not a punitive event or a mere formality, but a genuine effort towards resolution and improvement. It reinforces accountability and builds long-term trust.

A Real Story: From Cold War to Collaboration

Consider the case of two team leads, let's call them Avesh and Swapnali, who oversaw interdependent functions. Their relationship had deteriorated into a cold war. Meetings were minefields of passive-aggressive remarks, emails were formal and guarded, and collaboration between their teams had ground to a halt, impacting project delivery and morale. The tension was palpable.

Recognizing the damage, I met with Avesh and Swapnali separately. Avesh felt Swapnali was constantly making decisions that impacted his team without consulting him, leading to chaos. Swapnali felt Avesh was resistant to change and unwilling to adapt his team's processes, making her team's work harder. Their perspectives, while valid to them, were siloed and based on assumptions born from lack of communication.

I then facilitated a joint conversation, setting ground rules for respectful dialogue. The initial moments were thick with unspoken tension. I had to actively guide them back to the agreed-upon rules, reminding them to focus on specific situations and use "I" statements.

As they began to truly listen to each other's experiences – listening with the intent to understand, not just to reply – the defensiveness slowly began to crack. Avesh expressed his frustration about feeling blindsided, which Swapnali heard as a need for clearer communication channels. Swapnali shared her pressure to meet tight deadlines, which Avesh heard as a need for more proactive information sharing from his team.

The conversation was not a single magical fix, but it was the crucial turning point. Over the next few weeks, facilitated by agreed-upon changes like a shared weekly planning sync and a clear protocol for cross-team decisions, their interactions began to thaw. They started communicating proactively, asking for input, and even brainstorming solutions together. The passive aggression disappeared, replaced by direct, respectful communication. Their teams, sensing the shift, also began collaborating more effectively.

Avesh and Swapnali were not bad colleagues; they were disconnected and operating under unresolved tensions. The difficult conversation, though uncomfortable, didn't break their relationship; it provided the necessary friction to clear the air, deepen their understanding of each other's challenges, and ultimately forge a stronger, more collaborative partnership. It was a transformation born directly from the courage to confront the conflict head-on.

Speak the Truth, Stay Kind, Stay Committed

Difficult conversations and conflicts are not pleasant detours on the path of leadership. They are integral parts of the journey. They are signals – indicators that something needs attention, adjustment, empathy, or a fundamental change in approach.

As a people manager, your responsibility is not to create an environment free of ripples, but to become a skilled navigator of the waves. It requires the courage to lean into discomfort, the clarity to identify the real issues, the preparation to approach thoughtfully, the humility to listen deeply, and the empathy to connect human-to-human, even when discussing difficult subjects.

It's about initiating those hard conversations with clear intent and compassion. It's about choosing your words carefully, grounding feedback in behavior, managing your own emotions, and knowing when to pause or seek help. It's about staying committed to finding resolution, even when it's challenging, and following through on commitments made.

When you consistently demonstrate the ability to navigate conflict with integrity and skill, your team learns they can trust you – not just with decisions, but with their vulnerability, their concerns, and their disagreements. They learn that conflict, while uncomfortable, can be a pathway to stronger relationships and better outcomes. And in that environment of trust and psychological safety, true team cohesion and transformation become genuinely possible.

I feel I should end this chapter with a story of a tough conversation I had with one of my ex-team members, let's call her Aaliya. I genuinely believed I had poured a lot into her professional growth during her time on my team, so it came as a surprise when she decided to leave without a proper conversation. I was undeniably upset by her decision, yet I chose not to express my feelings at the time. Over the years, many people have moved on from my team, and I've always maintained a strong rapport with them, ensuring they feel supported whenever they reach out. But with Aaliya, something was different.

Later, when she called me for some help and guidance, I realized, with a pang of regret, that my usual warmth wasn't there. It bothered me, especially as I was writing this very chapter. So, I picked up the phone and called her immediately to apologize. Her response warmed my heart – she genuinely said she hadn't felt any rudeness. Still, the act of reaching out, of choosing to settle things rather than letting an unresolved feeling linger, brought a sense of peace and reinforced the profound importance of authentic connection, even after the professional paths diverge.

"When we avoid difficult conversations, we trade short-term discomforts for long-term dysfunction." – Peter Bromberg

Chapter **13**

Negotiation Skills for People Managers

"Let us never negotiate out of fear. But let us never fear to negotiate." – John F Kennedy

In the bustling theatre of the modern workplace, where priorities shift like sand and human dynamics are in constant motion, the ability to navigate differences and reach harmonious agreements is not merely an advantage – it's the very bedrock of effective leadership. While the term "negotiation" might conjure images of high-stakes corporate mergers or complex labor disputes, for those who lead teams, it's a skill woven into the fabric of their daily interactions. This chapter is dedicated to exploring the nuanced, vital role of negotiation for people managers, illustrating how this fundamental competency underpins trust, drives results, and shapes a positive team environment.

Why Negotiation is a Core Managerial Skill: Beyond the Boardroom

Step back from the traditional perception of negotiation as a formal, often adversarial process confined to boardrooms and legal contracts. For a people manager, negotiation lives in the heartbeat of the team. It's in the morning stand-up when competing task priorities must be reconciled. It's in the one-on-one when career aspirations meet business realities. It's in the cross-functional meeting where resource needs clash.

At its heart, managerial negotiation is about understanding, aligning, and influencing interests. It's a dynamic process involving listening, communicating, empathizing, and problem-solving, all aimed at reaching mutually acceptable outcomes. It's the art of finding common ground, even when starting from different positions. It's about guiding individuals and the team towards shared objectives while respecting individual needs and fostering strong relationships. You're not just negotiating for something; you're often negotiating with someone you need to collaborate with long after the current conversation ends. Your ability to do so with clarity, integrity, and genuine empathy doesn't just determine the immediate outcome; it profoundly impacts trust, morale, and long-term productivity.

Everyday Moments: The Unseen Negotiations of Leadership

As a people manager, you're a constant, often subtle, negotiator. Recognizing this transforms how you approach your role. It shifts your perspective from simply making decisions or giving directives to engaging in collaborative problem-solving.

Consider these commonplace scenarios, each a distinct form of managerial negotiation:

- Time-Off Requests During Crunch Time: A critical project deadline looms, and a valued team member requests leave for a significant personal event. This is not just an administrative approval; it's a negotiation. You need to balance the individual's valid need for rest/personal time with the team's commitment and the project's success. This involves discussing potential handover, adjusting timelines, exploring partial availability, or finding temporary support.
- Performance Feedback and Development: Sharing feedback, especially constructive criticism, involves navigating differing perspectives. Your assessment meets their self-perception and aspirations. Negotiating here is about aligning on the current reality, agreeing on areas for growth, setting actionable goals,

and determining the support needed. It's a negotiation about the path forward, balancing performance requirements with developmental opportunities.

- Role Evolution and Promotions: When a team member seeks more responsibility, a change in focus, or a promotion, it triggers a negotiation around expectations, required skills, timelines, and potential compensation. It's a dialogue about their value, their potential, and how it aligns with the team's evolving needs and organizational structure.

- Resource Allocation: Within your team or across departments, assigning limited resources – be it budget, headcount, or even just your own time and attention – often requires negotiation. Who gets priority? How are tasks distributed fairly while leveraging individual strengths?

- Conflict Resolution: When disagreements arise between team members or with stakeholders, the manager often steps in as a facilitator, helping parties negotiate their way to a resolution. This involves understanding competing interests, managing emotions, and guiding them towards a mutually acceptable compromise or solution.

Even in seemingly simple interactions – discussing a deadline, assigning a task, clarifying expectations – there's an element of aligning understanding and gaining buy-in, which are fundamental aspects of negotiation. Recognizing this embedded negotiation makes you more deliberate, proactive, and skilled in handling these critical daily interactions.

I reside in the vibrant city of Kolkata, India, a place where community and festivals hold immense significance. One of the most prominent events is Durga Puja, celebrated with unparalleled fervor around October. This five-day festival presents a recurring, fascinating case study in managerial negotiation. For my team members, it's a deeply important time for family, worship, and celebration. They need to be present for these moments. Yet, as managers in the service delivery industry, our commitment to clients and deliverables remains unwavering, 24/7.

Here, the annual Durga Puja leave negotiation unfolds. It's a masterclass in finding the 'win-win'. Managers understand the cultural imperative and the emotional need to celebrate. Team members understand the professional responsibility. The negotiation isn't about if people can take leave, but how we can collectively ensure continuity. This involves creative scheduling: some team members might negotiate for staggered leave across the five days, others for intense work during non-peak festival hours (late nights or early mornings), some might take full leave for 2-3 core days and work full shifts on others, while others might negotiate for the ability to work remotely, balancing family visits with quick check-ins or essential tasks. The outcome is not a standardized rule enforced from the top; it's a series of individual and team-level agreements reached through open dialogue, flexibility, and a shared commitment to both cultural values and work responsibilities. This dynamic is replicated across India for various festivals and is a powerful reminder that successful managerial negotiation is deeply human, context-aware, and focused on practical solutions that honor both individual needs and collective goals.

The Mindset: Embracing Collaborative Negotiation

The word "negotiation" can sometimes carry a competitive connotation – "winning" vs. "losing." This perspective can be paralyzing for managers who fear being overly aggressive (and damaging relationships) or overly passive (and failing to meet objectives). However, effective managerial negotiation is fundamentally collaborative.

A collaborative negotiator operates from a place of seeking mutual benefit. Their goal isn't to "win" at the other person's expense, but to find an outcome where everyone involved feels heard, respected, and reasonably satisfied. They understand that in the context of managing people, the relationship is as important as the immediate outcome, if not more so.

This mindset shift involves:

- Focusing on Interests, Not Positions: Instead of getting fixated on a stated demand ("I need these exact three days off"), a collaborative negotiator explores the underlying interest ("I need to spend quality time with my family during the core festival days"). Understanding the 'why' behind a request unlocks alternative solutions that might satisfy the core need without necessarily conceding the initial position.
- Belief in Joint Problem-Solving: Viewing the situation not as a conflict, but as a challenge to be solved together. "How can we ensure both the project deadline is met and you get to celebrate Durga Puja?" frames it as a shared objective.
- Commitment to Long-Term Relationships: Recognizing that today's negotiation sets the stage for future interactions. A heavy-handed or dismissive approach might yield a short-term gain but can erode trust and make future collaboration significantly harder.

Adopting this collaborative mindset doesn't mean being a pushover. It means approaching discussions with curiosity, empathy, and a genuine desire to find workable solutions, while also being clear about your own constraints and needs.

Preparing for High-Stakes Conversations

Few managerial negotiations are truly "low-stakes" when you consider their impact on individual motivation and team dynamics. Therefore, preparation is not a luxury; it's a necessity. This doesn't mean scripting a rigid dialogue, but rather engaging in thoughtful anticipation and clear self-reflection.

Effective preparation involves multiple layers:

- Define Your Objectives Clearly: What is the ideal outcome for you, the team, and the organization? What are the non-negotiables? What are your priorities? Knowing your desired end-point provides a compass for the conversation.

- Understand Your BATNA (Best Alternative to a Negotiated Agreement): What will you do if an agreement cannot be reached? Having a clear alternative gives you strength and prevents you from accepting an unfavorable deal out of desperation. Similarly, consider their potential BATNA.

- Anticipate the Other Person's Perspective: This is where empathy becomes a strategic tool. Put yourself in their shoes. What are their likely objectives, concerns, fears, and motivations? What pressures are they under? What are their potential alternatives? The more you understand their world, the better you can frame your proposals and address their potential reservations.

- Identify Potential Options and Concessions: Brainstorm various ways the negotiation could be resolved. What are you willing to offer or concede? What creative solutions might exist that haven't been discussed yet? Having a range of possibilities makes you more flexible and resourceful.

- Understand the Constraints: Be clear about the external factors limiting the negotiation – budget, policy, timelines, client demands. Transparency about these constraints is crucial, but focus on problem-solving within them, rather than using them as excuses.

- Emotional Readiness: Negotiation, especially on sensitive topics like performance or role changes, can be emotionally charged. Prepare yourself mentally. Stay grounded. Be aware of your own triggers or biases. Decide how you'll handle potential frustration, disappointment, or resistance with composure. Inner clarity projects outer confidence and presence. Knowing your core values in the situation helps you remain centered.

By investing time in this multi-faceted preparation, you move into the conversation feeling more confident, adaptable, and ready to engage constructively, rather than simply reacting to what comes your way.

Listening as a Strategic Advantage

In the heat of a negotiation, there's a strong urge to advocate for your position, to speak persuasively. Yet, the most powerful tool in a skilled negotiator's arsenal is not their voice, but their ears. I find myself returning to the paramount importance of listening time and again because it's fundamental to effective communication and, by extension, to successful negotiation.

When you truly listen – actively and empathetically – you gain invaluable insights. You pick up on subtle cues: hesitation in their voice, a repeated phrase that signals an underlying worry, an emotional undertone that reveals the true significance of their request. You move beyond the surface-level "what" they are asking for to the deeper "why."

As a manager, this deep listening gives you the power to:

- Identify Underlying Interests: When a team member pushes hard for a specific training course, listening might reveal their interest isn't just the course itself, but a desire for increased visibility or a fear of being left behind technologically.
- Build Trust: Listening attentively without interrupting or formulating your rebuttal shows respect. It signals that you value their perspective, making them more open to hearing yours.
- Discover Unstated Needs: Sometimes, the most important information is what isn't being said. Active listening, combined with open-ended questions, can uncover hidden concerns or motivations.
- Reframe the Discussion: Armed with a deeper understanding, you can reframe the conversation in a way that resonates. Instead of arguing against a specific request, you might say, "It sounds

like your core need here is growth and feeling equipped for future challenges. Let's explore a few different ways we can achieve that, beyond just this specific training." This shifts the focus from a potential point of contention to a shared goal.

Listening is not a passive activity. It requires focus, the suppression of your own immediate responses, and a genuine curiosity about the other person's reality. In negotiation, it's the process of gathering the intelligence needed to find the best path forward, together.

Balancing Assertiveness and Empathy

One of the common tightropes managers walk in negotiation is finding the right balance between advocating for their needs and the team's objectives (assertiveness) and acknowledging and respecting the other person's feelings and perspective (empathy). Leaning too far one way leads to being perceived as demanding or insensitive; leaning too far the other leads to being seen as weak or easily swayed.

The sweet spot lies in assertive empathy. This is the ability to clearly and confidently state your position, needs, and constraints while simultaneously demonstrating a genuine understanding and respect for the other person's feelings, situation, and point of view.

Practically, this looks like:

Starting by acknowledging their position or emotion: "I understand that taking these specific days off for the festival is incredibly important to you, and I appreciate you raising it."

Clearly stating your position and the reasons behind it: "...And I also need us to consider the critical project deadline we have and the impact on the team if coverage isn't maintained."

Using "I" statements to express your needs without blaming: "I feel concerned about our ability to meet the client's expectations if we don't have sufficient resources during that period."

Focusing on shared reality or constraints: "Given the client commitment and the current staffing levels, here's what we need to ensure..."

Inviting collaboration on finding a solution: "How can we work together to find a way for you to participate in the celebrations while ensuring our deliverables aren't negatively impacted?"

Being assertive doesn't mean being aggressive or cold. It means being clear, direct, and confident in stating your needs and boundaries. Being empathetic doesn't mean agreeing with everything the other person says or giving in to their demands. It means listening, acknowledging their feelings, and showing that you value them as an individual, even when you have differing views or constraints. This balance builds immense credibility and fosters a climate of mutual respect, making future negotiations significantly smoother. People are more likely to collaborate with and concede to someone they perceive as firm but fair.

Dealing With Resistance and Emotion

Not all negotiations proceed smoothly. You'll inevitably encounter resistance, frustration, disappointment, or even overt anger. These moments are perhaps the truest test of a manager's negotiation skill and emotional intelligence.

When faced with strong emotions:

- Prioritize De-escalation: Your primary goal initially is to prevent the situation from becoming adversarial or shutting down communication. Remain calm, even if the other person is not. Your composure can be an anchor.
- Listen and Acknowledge: Allow the other person to express their feelings without interruption. Don't get defensive. Simply listen. Once they've finished, acknowledge their emotion without necessarily agreeing with their perspective. Phrases like, "I can see you're feeling very frustrated about this," or "It sounds

like this situation is causing you a lot of stress," validate their experience and can help diffuse intensity. Sometimes, people just need to feel heard before they can move forward.

- Seek Understanding, Not Agreement: Ask open-ended questions to understand the source of their emotion. "What specifically about this situation is most frustrating for you?" or "Help me understand your biggest concern here."

- Take a Break if Necessary: If emotions are running too high, it's perfectly acceptable to suggest pausing the conversation and resuming later when everyone has had a chance to cool down. "I can see this is upsetting, and I want us to have a productive conversation. Perhaps we can take a break and revisit this in an hour/tomorrow?"

- Re-focus on Shared Goals: Once emotions have settled slightly, gently steer the conversation back to the objective reality and the shared goals you both ostensibly have. "We both want [positive outcome]. How can we work together to overcome this challenge?" Reframe obstacles as problems you can solve collaboratively.

Navigating emotion gracefully means not taking it personally, not retaliating, and not letting it derail the search for a solution. It's about being the steady presence that helps guide the conversation back to productive ground.

Negotiating Within Constraints: Finding Value in Limitation

As a manager, you rarely operate with unlimited resources or complete autonomy. You'll frequently find yourself negotiating within defined constraints – budget limits, organizational policies, headcount freezes, fixed timelines, or client requirements. These limitations are not necessarily roadblocks to negotiation, but rather parameters within which creativity must flourish.

In these situations, honesty and transparency about the constraints are crucial. Avoid vague excuses or blaming "management." Instead, clearly explain the limitations you're working within: "Due to the regulatory requirements, we have a hard deadline that we cannot shift."

The negotiation then shifts from challenging the constraint itself to finding value within the constraint. This requires creativity and a focus on the underlying interests.

If a deadline is fixed: Can you negotiate for additional temporary resources, a reduction in scope elsewhere, prioritization of this work over other tasks, or increased support from other departments? Negotiate for the resources or conditions needed to meet the constraint.

If headcount is frozen: Can you negotiate for technology solutions to improve efficiency, outsourcing specific tasks, or redefining roles within the existing team?

Negotiation within constraints is about exploring the full spectrum of potential value, not just the most obvious forms. It's about being realistic about what's possible while being imaginative about how to still meet core needs and objectives. It teaches you and your team to be resourceful problem-solvers.

Internal Negotiation: Managing Up and Across the Organization

Managerial negotiation is not limited to interactions with your direct team members. A significant part of your role involves navigating relationships and influencing outcomes with individuals over whom you have no direct authority: your own manager and peers in other departments.

Managing Up: Negotiating with your manager involves advocating for your team's needs – be it for resources, protection from excessive demands, career development opportunities, or strategic direction.

This requires understanding your manager's priorities, the broader organizational goals, and the constraints they are operating under. Successful "managing up" in a negotiation context means:

- Framing your requests in terms of how they benefit the business or align with senior leadership's objectives.
- Coming prepared with data and a clear rationale.
- Offering solutions, not just presenting problems.
- Being receptive to their feedback and alternative suggestions.
- Knowing when to push and when to accept a decision.

It's about building a partnership based on mutual respect and shared goals.

Collaborating effectively with peers in other departments often requires negotiation, especially when priorities or resources conflict. You have no formal authority over them, so influence becomes paramount.

Half a decade ago, I faced a significant challenge: managing the ramp-down of a process involving over 300 resources. This was a difficult situation, requiring the redeployment of a large number of people. Finding suitable roles for everyone within a tight timeframe was a monumental task that absolutely necessitated extensive internal negotiation with managers from other projects and departments who had potential openings.

What made this complex negotiation successful was not a top-down mandate, but strong collaboration with my peers. I invested time in understanding their projects' needs, timelines, and skill requirements. I proactively shared information about the resources available, highlighting their skills and potential fit. The negotiations involved matching skills, discussing onboarding timelines, agreeing on temporary assignments, and sometimes creatively adjusting role requirements slightly to accommodate available talent. It was a process of give-and-take, built on existing relationships and a shared understanding of the organizational need to retain talent and manage the transition smoothly. By focusing on mutual benefit – other projects gaining skilled resources, my team members finding new roles, the organization retaining valuable employees – we were able to navigate a potentially disruptive situation. The success was a direct result of collaborative negotiation with peers, demonstrating that even in challenging circumstances, finding common ground and working together leads to better outcomes for everyone involved. We gradually finalized placements, and remarkably, things concluded with a sense of relief and even smiles, a testament to the power of respectful, collaborative internal negotiation.

Managing across requires building rapport, understanding your peers' pressures, finding areas of mutual benefit, and focusing on the collective success of the organization rather than departmental turf wars.

Building a Negotiation Culture in Your Team: A Legacy of Collaboration

Your behavior as a manager sets the tone for your team. How you handle disagreements, make decisions, and interact with others in situations requiring negotiation sends powerful signals. If you model calm, clear, and fair negotiation, your team will learn from it and are more likely to adopt similar approaches in their own interactions, both internally and externally.

Cultivating a negotiation culture within your team involves:

- Open Communication: Encourage team members to express their needs, concerns, and perspectives openly and constructively. Create a safe space for dialogue.
- Coaching and Guidance: Explicitly coach your team on how to approach difficult conversations. Teach them the principles of focusing on interests, active listening, and finding win-win solutions.

- Empowerment: Empower team members to negotiate solutions directly when appropriate, rather than always escalating issues to you. Trust them to find common ground.
- Celebrating Collaborative Outcomes: Acknowledge and celebrate when team members successfully negotiate solutions among themselves or with stakeholders, reinforcing the value of this approach.
- Leading by Example: Be transparent about your own negotiation processes (where appropriate) and demonstrate the behaviors you want to see.

A team that understands and practices negotiation with integrity is more resilient, better equipped to handle conflict, more collaborative, and ultimately, more effective in achieving its goals.

A Real-Life Scenario: Negotiation Without Noise

The shift to remote work post-pandemic presented managers with a new set of challenges, including maintaining quality and focus outside the traditional office environment. In one specific process I managed, a noticeable decline in quality coincided with a significant portion of the team working from home. Client feedback highlighted this drop, creating a situation that demanded a thoughtful, negotiated response, rather than a simple directive to return to the office.

We recognized the genuine reasons many preferred working from home – flexibility, reduced commute, personal circumstances. However, we also had a critical business need: improved quality. The negotiation wasn't about revoking work-from-home entirely, but about linking it to performance and finding a mutual path to improvement.

The approach was framed as a negotiation based on performance and trust. We communicated the problem clearly to the affected team members – the client feedback and the correlation observed with working from home. We acknowledged their preference for remote work. Then, we presented the proposed solution as a conditional agreement: those with quality issues would be required to return to the office for a certain period, say one quarter. This was not a punishment, but an opportunity to re-establish focus and leverage the immediate support and collaboration the office environment provides. The crucial part of the negotiation was the caveat: if they demonstrably improved their quality scores during this quarter in the office, we would re-negotiate the work arrangement, allowing them to return to working from home provided they maintained that improved level of quality going forward.

This approach was perceived as fair because it clearly linked the work arrangement to a measurable outcome (quality) and offered a path back to their preferred model based on performance. It wasn't a permanent restriction, but a temporary adjustment with a clear goal and a potential return to flexibility. This sensitized the team members to the importance of quality even while remote, encouraged them to leverage the in-office period effectively, and ultimately, led to improved quality scores. It was a successful negotiation because it addressed the business need while respecting the team's preferences, finding a balanced outcome that everyone could understand and commit to – a true "negotiation without noise," achieving results through clear conditions and mutual agreement rather than conflict.

Negotiation and Self-Advocacy

While focusing on negotiating effectively with and for your team is paramount, it's also essential to remember that managers must sometimes negotiate for themselves. Many managers, comfortable advocating for others, hesitate when it comes to their own career progression, resource needs, or work-life balance.

Self-advocacy is not about being demanding or entitled; it's about clearly articulating your value, your needs, and your aspirations with humility and strength. It's about initiating conversations about your career path, negotiating for the resources you need to enable your team's success, or discussing flexible work arrangements for yourself if needed.

When you, as a manager, effectively negotiate for your own needs in a professional, well-reasoned manner, you role-model healthy self-advocacy. You demonstrate to your team that it's acceptable and necessary to speak up for oneself, to articulate value, and to actively participate in shaping one's career and work environment. This reinforces the idea that negotiation is not about being difficult, but about being clear, prepared, and respectful in pursuing your goals.

Influence With Integrity: The Enduring Goal

Ultimately, the essence of managerial negotiation is not about power or manipulation. It's about influence built on integrity. It's the process of clarifying different needs, finding shared interests, and constructing agreements that are not only functional but also durable because they are founded on mutual understanding and respect.

Every conversation you have as a people manager holds the potential for negotiation – whether it's about tasks, timelines, expectations, feelings, or futures. Approaching these moments with a collaborative mindset, thorough preparation, deep listening, balanced communication, and emotional intelligence enables you to negotiate wisely.

The most effective managers don't necessarily "win" every point in a negotiation. They don't seek to overpower or outsmart. Instead, they seek outcomes that strengthen relationships, build trust, and lay the groundwork for continued collaboration. They walk away from the table not having taken the most, but having earned respect. As Satya

Nadella thoughtfully articulated in "Hit Refresh," the focus should be on creating shared value, moving beyond the zero-sum game mentality. Successful managerial negotiation is about expanding the pie, not just dividing it.

"The ability to negotiate with other people without friction and argument is the outstanding quality of all successful people."
– Napolean Hill

Part V

Looking Ahead

CHAPTER 14

The Evolving Role of the People Manager

"They always say time changes things, but you actually have to change them yourself." – Andy Warhol

The truth of Warhol's words echoes louder than ever in the landscape of modern work. We are not passive observers of change; we are its architects, especially those of us in positions to guide and support others. The familiar office corridors, once echoing with synchronous footsteps and the clatter of keyboards, have stretched into virtual spaces and hybrid models. The workforce itself is a vibrant, complex tapestry, woven with threads from multiple generations, each bringing unique colors, textures, and expectations. Technology doesn't just support our work; it fundamentally alters how we connect, collaborate, and create.

In this exciting, sometimes disorienting, new world, the blueprint for leadership has been redrawn. The manager's role, once primarily focused on process, output, and directive, has undergone a profound metamorphosis. It's no longer about merely managing tasks; it's about cultivating people. We've shifted from being administrative overseers to becoming architects of human potential, building environments where individuals and teams don a sense of trust, purpose, and genuine belonging. This is not just an evolution; it's a revolution in leadership, demanding not just a different skillset, but a different mindset, one grounded in empathy, authenticity, and courage.

From Overseer to Enabler

The traditional manager-subordinate dynamic, a relic of industrial-era hierarchies, is rapidly dissolving. The command-and-control structure, where instructions flowed downwards and execution upwards, stifles the very innovation and agility needed today. High-performing teams in the modern era don't thrive under constant surveillance; they flourish in an atmosphere of trust. They crave autonomy within clear boundaries, ownership over their contributions, and the psychological safety to experiment, fail, and learn without fear of punitive repercussions.

This transition from task-master to trust-builder is the true alchemy of modern management. It's less about watching people work and more about enabling them to do their best work. It involves moving from the granular oversight of 'what' and 'how' to fostering the 'why' and empowering the 'who'. A great manager today doesn't just assign a task; they provide context, clarify the desired outcome, offer resources, and then step back, trusting their team members to navigate the path. This is not abdication; it's empowerment born of belief.

Building this kind of trust is not achieved through policy mandates or periodic team-building exercises alone. It's forged in the small, consistent moments of interaction. It's in demonstrating genuine empathy – not just saying "I understand," but truly listening to understand someone's challenges, frustrations, or aspirations. It's in the unwavering consistency of your actions aligning with your words – walking the talk, always. People aren't checking your project dashboards; they are scanning for authenticity and care. The silent question echoing in the hearts of many employees today, particularly the younger generation, is: "Does my manager genuinely care about me as a person, beyond my deliverables?" The answer to that question is the bedrock of engagement, loyalty, and discretionary effort.

And yes, as I mentioned before, this connection is a two-way street. While the manager must initiate and model this culture of care, it requires reciprocation from the team. However, the onus to set the tone, to extend the initial gesture of trust and vulnerability, undeniably rests with the leader. It's about planting the seed and nurturing the soil, creating an environment where mutual care can grow.

Understanding the Modern Soul

Our teams are richer and more complex than ever, representing a vibrant mosaic of generational experiences. We have team members who navigated dial-up internet alongside those who grew up with smartphones in their hands. Leading across this spectrum – from the seasoned wisdom of Baby Boomers and Gen X, to the digital fluency of Millennials, and the purpose-driven authenticity of Gen Z – requires a nuanced and adaptable approach. Some value stability forged over years, others seek rapid impact and flexible pathways. Communication preferences vary wildly – some prefer formal emails; others thrive on quick chat messages or even a well-placed meme.

Viewing this diversity as a challenge is a missed opportunity. It's, in fact, our greatest strength. It's a fertile ground for innovation, a natural incubator for diverse perspectives, and a constant invitation to grow as leaders. It demands personalized leadership – not favoritism, but a willingness to understand individual motivations, communication styles, and career aspirations, tailoring our support accordingly.

This is where I've found a profound connection, particularly with the Gen Z members of my teams. They are often characterized by their desire for authenticity, their unwavering focus on mental well-being, their need for clear and frequent feedback, their skepticism towards traditional corporate norms, and a deep yearning for their work to have meaning and societal impact. My approach, which has always prioritized genuine human connection, transparency (within professional bounds), open conversations about challenges (both professional and the human element behind them), and a visible passion for finding purpose in our work, seems to resonate deeply with this generation.

Instead of assuming what motivates them, I've learned to simply ask. I've spent countless hours in 1:1s, not just reviewing tasks, but listening – truly listening – to their stories, their anxieties about the future, their ideas for making things better, their perspective on the world. I've embraced their digital fluency, sometimes even learning from them about new tools or communication styles. When they speak about mental health concerns, I don't dismiss it; I validate their feelings and explore how we, as a team and an organization, can create a more supportive environment. When they question traditional processes, I invite them to propose alternatives. This openness, this willingness to see them not just as employees but as individuals with unique insights and valid concerns, seems to cut through the hierarchical noise that many younger professionals are wary of. They see a leader who is relatable, human, and genuinely invested in their well-being and growth, not just their output. It's less about being "popular" in a superficial sense, and more about building mutual respect and understanding through authentic engagement.

Having had the privilege of working alongside Baby Boomers, Gen X, Millennials, and now Gen Z, my leadership journey has been immensely enriched. Each interaction has deepened my understanding of diverse motivations and communication styles. I eagerly anticipate the insights that Gen Alphas will bring, and who knows, perhaps even Gen Betas. This continuous engagement with evolving perspectives isn't just a professional necessity, but a profound and rewarding aspect of modern leadership.

The Symphony of Data and Heart

The digital age provides managers with an unprecedented flood of data – performance metrics, project timelines, collaboration tool activity logs. This data is invaluable; it can highlight trends, identify bottlenecks, and inform decisions. But data alone is a sterile narrative. It can tell you what happened, but rarely why. A dashboard might flag a dip in productivity, but it can't tell you if that dip is due to a personal crisis, burnout, a lack of necessary resources, or a fundamental misunderstanding of the goal.

The art of modern management lies in conducting a symphony between the analytical insights provided by data and the rich, complex human narrative that underpins them. Great managers use data as a compass to guide conversations, not as a hammer to enforce compliance. They see metrics as prompts for curiosity: "This data suggests X is happening. Let's talk about your experience and understand what's truly going on."

I've consistently championed the importance of maintaining a strong human connection, often against advice that suggested it could lead to people bypassing the chain of command or that I'd be overwhelmed by minor issues. The counsel often sounded practical on the surface: "Maintain professional distance," "Don't be too approachable." But I fundamentally disagreed. While I would never encourage bypassing legitimate reporting lines for professional issues that their direct manager could resolve, I firmly believe that fostering a culture where people feel safe and comfortable reaching out as individuals, to share a concern, ask for guidance on a non-work-related stressor, or simply feel seen, is paramount.

This belief stemmed from a simple truth I observed over years: real, sustainable success in a team doesn't come from rigid control; it comes from authentic connection. It was through these open channels, these moments of genuine human interaction – the informal chat, the quick check-in beyond the project update, the willingness to talk about life outside of work – that I gained the crucial insights. I saw the silent struggles hidden behind brave faces. I could celebrate a small, personal victory that wasn't visible on any performance report. I created a space where doubt and vulnerability weren't weaknesses, but necessary steps towards growth. And it was in learning from my team members – their diverse experiences, their unique strengths, their resilient spirits honed by past challenges – that I truly grew as a leader, far more than any management textbook could teach me. This approach particularly resonates with Gen Z, who often prioritize authenticity and value leaders who are relatable and show genuine care beyond the professional facade.

Leading with Compassion

Perhaps the most significant and necessary shift in management consciousness over the past decade is the long-overdue acknowledgment of mental health in the workplace. Burnout, anxiety, stress – these are not abstract concepts or character flaws; they are realities that impact our teams' ability to function and thrive. The expectation that employees must compartmentalize their emotional lives and leave them at the office door (or log-off screen) is not only unrealistic but actively harmful.

Today's manager doesn't need a psychology degree, but they absolutely must possess emotional intelligence and courage. Courage to have difficult conversations, to ask probing questions, and to create an environment where people feel safe admitting they are struggling. Being an emotionally aware leader means recognizing the subtle signs of stress or withdrawal, initiating check-ins that go beyond "How's the project?", and actively encouraging team members to prioritize self-care without fear of judgment or negative repercussions. It also means modeling this behavior ourselves – acknowledging our own need for breaks, setting boundaries, and being open about our own moments of vulnerability (appropriately, of course).

I have witnessed, with deep concern, managers who dismiss mental health concerns, particularly from younger employees, often resorting to dismissive platitudes like, "They are not serious about their jobs," or "Back in my day..." This perspective is not only outdated; it's damaging. It creates a chasm of mistrust and alienation, leaving employees feeling unheard and unsupported. It reinforces a toxic culture where showing any sign of struggle is perceived as weakness. These managers then wonder why they struggle with engagement or retention, blind to the fact that they are actively dismantling the human connection essential for team cohesion.

Conversely, I've observed that the increased openness about mental health among Gen Z, while sometimes manifesting in ways that older generations might not immediately understand (like vocalizing feeling overwhelmed without a single, clear external stressor), is a positive step. It's an invitation for dialogue. While I agree with the perspective that excessive digital stimulation and the resulting dopamine dysregulation can be a contributing factor to feelings of anxiety or lack of focus, pointing this out should be done with empathy and support, not judgment. Cal Newport is his highly acclaimed book "Digital Minimalism" advocates that the Managers can play a role by fostering environments conducive to deep work, encouraging digital minimalism during focus times, and helping team members develop strategies for managing digital distractions. Crucially, validating how someone feels, even if the cause is complex, is the first step to helping them navigate it. My willingness to listen without judgment, to share resources (without acting as a therapist), and to simply create a safe space for these conversations has been a significant factor in building trust with my Gen Z colleagues, who appreciate being taken seriously when they speak about their well-being. They see that I value them as people, not just producers.

DEI: Weaving the Fabric of Belonging

Diversity, Equity, and Inclusion are no longer optional add-ons or initiatives confined to the HR department. They are fundamental pillars of effective modern leadership. Every decision a manager makes, no matter how small it seems – who is assigned to a high-visibility project, who is asked to speak up in a meeting, who receives informal mentorship – either reinforces existing biases or actively builds a more equitable and inclusive environment.

An inclusive manager is a conscious leader who actively challenges their own assumptions and biases. They understand that "equal treatment" doesn't always equate to "equitable opportunity." They make a deliberate effort to ensure that quieter voices are heard and amplified, not drowned out by the most dominant personalities. They actively cultivate psychological safety, creating a space where everyone feels not just tolerated, but genuinely belongs, valued for their unique perspectives and experiences. This is not achieved through diversity training alone, but through consistent, intentional practice in daily interactions.

Moreover, the inclusive manager doesn't just navigate differences; they celebrate them as the vital fuel for creativity and innovation. In our VUCA (Volatile, Uncertain, Complex, Ambiguous) world, the best ideas often emerge from the intersection of different viewpoints and experiences. Leveraging technology to facilitate brainstorming, like the hackathons and ideathons I'm fortunate to be a part of in my organization, is powerful, but the technology is just a tool. True magic happens when everyone feels included and empowered to contribute their ideas, regardless of their role, background, or communication style. My experience in environments where every idea, from every corner, is genuinely considered and iterated upon has reinforced my belief that inclusivity is not just the right thing to do; it's a strategic imperative that unlocks unimaginable potential. It's about building a team where the collective is truly greater than the sum of its parts because every part is seen, valued, and integrated.

Igniting the Spark of Purpose

Beyond salaries and promotions, today's workforce, particularly younger generations, seeks meaning. They want to understand why their work matters, how it connects to a larger mission, and whether their organization and its leaders stand for something beyond the bottom line. The manager is the crucial link, the translator who connects the often-mundane reality of daily tasks to the inspiring vision of collective impact.

When a task feels repetitive or insignificant, a good leader doesn't just mandate its completion; they reframe it, highlighting its contribution to the broader goal. They connect the dots between the individual effort and the team's success, the company's mission, or even the impact on customers or society. When motivation wavers, they gently remind the team of the shared "why."

Purpose doesn't need to be a grand, abstract corporate slogan. It needs to be authentic and tangibly linked to values and impact. It begins with the leader's own sincerity and ability to articulate that connection. I recall a pivotal moment with my mentor, Abhishek Garg, in the summer of 2023. I had expressed a desire to deepen my understanding of the business beyond just delivery. We were in a car, a seemingly ordinary moment, but what he said next was transformational. Looking at me, he said, "Avisek, you've always wanted to understand the business finance side. Forget delivery for a moment. From tomorrow, you own the financial health of your account. You'll learn, you'll make mistakes, but you'll be responsible." This wasn't just a delegation; it was the assignment of a significant purpose. It elevated my role beyond managing tasks to stewarding a critical aspect of the business. My motivation soared because I was given a meaningful challenge that aligned with my aspirations and demonstrated trust in my potential. This experience solidified my understanding that one of the most powerful things a manager can do is connect an individual's work to a larger, meaningful objective.

Embracing the Learning Journey

In this constantly shifting landscape, the most effective managers are not those who project an image of knowing everything. They are the humble ones, the curious ones, the ones committed to a lifelong journey of learning, unlearning outdated models, and relearning new approaches. They understand that the half-life of knowledge is shrinking.

This commitment to learning manifests in various ways: voracious reading of books, articles, and research; actively soliciting and being receptive to feedback, even when it's difficult to hear; dedicating time for quiet reflection; observing other leaders and teams; and, crucially, possessing the humility to say, "I was wrong," or "I don't know, let's find out together." This willingness to be vulnerable about one's own learning process doesn't diminish authority; it builds trust and creates a culture where curiosity and growth are celebrated, not seen as admissions of weakness. Leadership is not about being the smartest person in the room; it's about fostering an environment where collective intelligence thrives through continuous learning and adaptation.

Even after nearly two decades in the professional world, I genuinely view myself as a perpetual fresher. The hunger to learn, to explore new ideas, to understand different perspectives, remains as strong as ever. Writing this very book has been a learning process, synthesizing countless insights from my experiences, conversations, and the work of others. My hope is that every reader, regardless of their experience level, finds something new to ponder in these pages, because the journey of learning in leadership, truly, has no stops and no final destination.

Leading Across the Digital Divide: Nurturing Connection in the Virtual Space

The widespread adoption of hybrid and remote work models has introduced a new layer of complexity to the manager's role. Building trust when interactions are primarily across screens, ensuring engagement when physical presence is absent, and fostering a sense of connection despite geographical distance require deliberate effort and creativity.

The evolving manager understands that "presence" in a virtual world is less about physical visibility and more about emotional availability and intentional connection. It's about ensuring team members feel seen, heard, and valued, even when they aren't physically co-located. This necessitates mastering asynchronous communication – using tools effectively to keep everyone informed and aligned without requiring constant real-time meetings. It demands creating new rituals of inclusion that translate to the virtual space – virtual coffee breaks, non-work-related chat channels, digital celebrations of milestones, and intentional "pulse checks" during 1:1s. The focus shifts from monitoring "online time" to measuring tangible output and impact. Above all, it means actively combating the potential for silence to be misinterpreted as disconnection; managers must proactively reach out, check in, and create safe spaces for communication.

During the height of the pandemic, when remote work became the unexpected norm, my role model Mr. Ramanarayana Parhi introduced a brilliant, simple concept: "Chai Pe Charcha" – discussion over a cup of tea. These were informal, monthly virtual gatherings with his team, with no agenda other than connecting as people. The magic was instantaneous. Team members who were often quiet or camera-shy in formal meetings opened up, shared stories, laughed, and built genuine rapport. I immediately adopted this theme for my own team, and the results were identical. It was a powerful reminder that even across screens, the fundamental human need for connection and informal interaction remains. While remote work presents unique challenges, the experience of the past few years has also equipped us with the creativity and understanding needed to bridge the digital divide and keep the human element central.

Cultivating Reflective Practice

In the relentless pace of modern work, managers can easily fall into the trap of simply reacting to the next urgent task, moving from one item to the next without pausing for breath. This constant forward momentum, without time for processing, leaves a residue of unexamined experiences and missed learning opportunities. The most impactful leaders understand the quiet power of reflection.

Reflection is not a luxury; it's a necessity. It's the practice of stepping back, not just to review what happened, but how it happened and how we showed up as leaders. It involves asking ourselves the difficult questions: Did I lead with compassion in that interaction? Was I truly inclusive in that meeting, or did I unintentionally silence a voice? Did I push my team too hard under pressure, or perhaps not provide enough clear direction? Did I react based on assumption rather than curiosity?

Reflection transforms raw experience into distilled wisdom. It allows us to identify patterns in our behavior, recognize our blind spots, celebrate what went well (and understand why), and pinpoint areas for growth. It's a practice that requires discipline – carving out quiet time amidst the chaos, whether through journaling, mindful walking, quiet contemplation, or discussing experiences with a trusted mentor or peer. This commitment to self-awareness and continuous improvement through reflection is what sustains effective leadership over the long haul.

The Manager of Tomorrow

The narrative that the manager's role is becoming obsolete in flatter organizations or the age of self-managing teams is fundamentally flawed. The need for human leadership is not diminishing; it's intensifying. The role is not fading away; it's being radically redefined and elevated in importance.

The manager of today, and certainly tomorrow, must be a multi-hyphenate leader: a strategic thinker who understands the business landscape, and a soft-skill expert fluent in empathy and communication; a performance driver focused on results, and a well-being champion who prioritizes the health of their team; a process optimizer who leverages technology, and a culture cultivator who builds belonging and psychological safety.

This sounds like a monumental task, and it's. But it's also an inspiring invitation – an invitation to lead with greater intention, deeper inclusion, and unwavering integrity. The evolving manager is not just someone who directs or oversees; they are someone who inspires potential, nurtures growth, fosters resilience, and fundamentally transforms not just the work their team does, but how their team members feel about themselves and their place in the world. It starts, as all true change does, with the leader's willingness to transform themselves first.

"The future belongs to those who adapt, learn, and lead through change." – Ravi Venkatesan

CHAPTER 15

The Unseen Monuments: Crafting a Legacy of Human Flourishing

"What you leave behind is not what is engraved in stone monuments, but what is woven into the lives of others." – Pericles

As the curtain begins to draw on a long and dedicated career, the reflective mind often drifts to a seemingly natural question: 'What monuments have I built? What tangible accolades mark my passage?' Yet, for the leader whose heart has been attuned to the subtle, profound music of human potential, a different, more resonant question echoes in the chambers of their conscience: 'Whose lives have I illuminated? Whose spirit did I help take flight?' For in the intricate, sprawling narrative of our professional existence, the ultimate testament to a leader's worth is not etched in the cold stone of statistical triumphs or the steel frames of completed projects. Instead, it's vibrantly alive, breathing and pulsing in the courage kindled in a hesitant heart, in the quiet dignity fiercely protected, in the resilience painstakingly nurtured within the souls they were privileged to guide.

This chapter, dear reader, doesn't seek to dissect the mechanics of management or the architecture of strategic frameworks. Those are but the tools, the scaffolding. We venture now into a more sacred space: the realm of legacy. We speak of the enduring essence that remains when the echoes of boardroom debates have faded, when the tyranny of deadlines has been silenced, and when the gilded nameplates on office doors are but a distant memory. We explore the indelible imprints, the luminous footprints a true people leader leaves upon the path of others – footprints that guide, inspire, and empower long after their own journey has taken a new turn.

The legacy of a people leader is not a static entry in an annual report or a carefully curated paragraph in a corporate history. It's a dynamic, living force. You'll find it not in laminated policies, but in the rekindled spark in the eyes of a team member who, once crippled by self-doubt, now dares to innovate, to stretch, to dream beyond the conventional. You'll hear it in the newfound timbre of a voice that, once muted by fear or insecurity, now articulates wisdom and conviction, unafraid to challenge, to contribute, to lead in their own right. It resides in the quiet strength of a colleague who, having weathered a personal or professional tempest, stands taller, more resolute, because you stood as their unwavering lighthouse, believing in their capacity to navigate the storm and reach calmer shores. This legacy is an echo in the laughter of a team that feels psychologically safe, a ripple in the collaborative energy of a group that trusts implicitly, a warmth in the shared memories of battles fought and won, not for individual glory, but for collective growth.

The acclaimed leadership thinker John C. Maxwell, in his seminal work "The 5 Levels of Leadership", articulates a profound journey culminating in "Pinnacle" leadership – Level 5. This is the sanctum of respect, a place where individuals follow not from obligation, nor for transactional benefit, but out of a deep, abiding admiration for who you're as a person and for the transformative impact you have had on their individual journeys. This, in its purest form, is the crucible of legacy. At this zenith, people do not merely recall your title or your hierarchical position; they remember your presence – the way you made them feel, the values you embodied, the unspoken lessons you imparted through your very being. They remember the integrity of your gaze, the empathy in your voice, the unwavering support in your stance.

Throughout my own odyssey in the world of work, I have observed the full spectrum of leadership. I have witnessed those who operated predominantly from Level 1 – Positional Power. Their teams moved, yes, but often with the mechanical compliance of those marching to orders, their steps heavy with obligation rather than inspired by conviction. These leaders were adept at managing deliverables, at ticking boxes, at ensuring the trains ran on time. But the hearts, the aspirations, the untapped reservoirs of potential within their people often remained fallow ground. Their legacy, if one could call it that, was often a sterile efficiency, devoid of warmth or lasting human connection.

Conversely, I have been profoundly blessed to walk alongside, and learn from, leaders who lived and breathed in the rarer atmospheres of Level 4 (People Development) and Level 5 (Pinnacle). These were the true cultivators of human potential. They poured their wisdom, their time, their genuine care into their people, not as a means to an end, but as an end in itself. They mentored without a hidden agenda, their guidance a sincere offering for growth. They led with a profound, almost fierce compassion, understanding that behind every employee ID was a universe of hopes, fears, dreams, and struggles. And the remarkable truth? These leaders rarely, if ever, needed to raise their voice or resort to the heavy hand of authority. Their impact, like a powerful undercurrent, moved people, inspired loyalty, and fostered excellence organically. Their legacy was woven into the very fabric of the organization's culture, visible in the thriving careers and confident spirits of those they had nurtured.

This kind of profound, lasting legacy is not forged in the grand, sweeping gestures often highlighted in leadership biographies. It's meticulously, lovingly constructed in the tapestry of a thousand "micro-moments" – those seemingly small, everyday interactions that, when infused with presence and genuine care, accumulate into a monumental impact. It's built in that crucial moment when you consciously choose to truly listen, to understand the unspoken, instead of impatiently lecturing or imposing your own narrative. It's cemented when you deflect the spotlight, ensuring that credit lands squarely on the deserving shoulders of your team members, rather than claiming their victories, however small, as your own. It's etched into the memory of your team when you stand as an advocate, a shield, for someone in the room who lacks the voice or the courage to speak for themselves, especially when it's unpopular or inconvenient to do so.

Consider the indelible mark left when you patiently, empathetically walked someone through the labyrinth of their self-doubt, not by offering platitudes, but by helping them uncover their own strength, their own solutions. Think of the loyalty engendered when you remembered the name of a team member's child who was facing surgery, not as a managerial tactic, but as a human being connecting with another. Reflect on the profound lesson in grace and growth offered when you forgave a significant mistake, not with a dismissive wave, but by transforming it into a powerful learning opportunity, thereby preserving dignity and fostering a culture where intelligent risk-taking is not punished. These are the sacred transactions where true leadership legacy is minted, moment by precious moment.

Satya Nadella, in his insightful narrative Hit Refresh, chronicles a monumental shift in the very DNA of a global behemoth, Microsoft. He understood that to revitalize such an institution, he couldn't merely enforce compliance through edicts or restructure through diagrams. He needed to inspire a cultural metamorphosis rooted in a deep, pervasive empathy. He led not by the dictates of an isolated ego, but through a profound commitment to understanding the perspectives, challenges, and aspirations of his people. In doing so, he did not just change a company; he began to sculpt a legacy of pervasive trust, genuine inclusion, and, as a direct consequence, unbridled innovation. He demonstrated that empathy is not a soft skill, but the bedrock of resilient, adaptive, and profoundly human organizations.

To embark on the path of building such a resonant legacy, a leader must undertake a fundamental shift in perspective – a conscious evolution from being a mere manager of performance to becoming a steward of human lives. It requires acknowledging that every individual who reports to you, collaborates with you, or is impacted by your decisions is far more than an employee ID or a functional resource. They are someone's cherished spouse, devoted parent, beloved sibling, or precious child. They arrive each day carrying an invisible backpack laden with personal hopes, private burdens, audacious dreams, and silent anxieties. Your words, carefully chosen or carelessly uttered, possess the power to shape the contours of their confidence, to bolster or brittle their self-belief. Your expressed trust acts as a crucible for their courage, empowering them to venture beyond their perceived limitations. Your feedback, when delivered with compassion, clarity, and a genuine intent to uplift, becomes not a judgment, but a precious catalyst for their ongoing growth and development.

As a people manager, you're not merely orchestrating tasks, overseeing projects, or ensuring targets are met. You're, in a very real and significant sense, shaping human trajectories. You're a co-author in the unfolding stories of their lives. This is a profound responsibility, and an even more profound privilege.

Decades from now, when the specifics of projects have blurred and the titles on business cards have long since faded, what will remain? People may forget the exact percentage of the sales target you exceeded, or the intricacies of the strategic plan you devised. But they will carry with them, with crystalline clarity, the memory of how you made them feel. They will remember, with enduring gratitude, if you stood as a steadfast anchor for them during a personal or professional storm, offering not just platitudes, but tangible support and unwavering belief. They will recall, with deep respect, if you possessed the grace and foresight to offer them a second chance after a stumble, understanding that failure is often the most potent teacher. They will cherish, for a lifetime, the memory of how you saw a nascent potential within them, a spark they themselves could not yet perceive, and how you fanned that spark into a flame.

I recently was blessed to realize the enduring power of these human connections when one of my closest family members was going through a very complicated medical procedure. During that incredibly tough time, my phone buzzed with messages and calls from many people with whom I no longer shared any working relationship. Yet, their genuine care, their prayers, and their heartfelt inquiries poured in like a soothing balm. One of these truly touching gestures came from Diptarco Singha, who had started his career in my team many years ago. He moved out of my team long back, but the warmth between us had clearly never faded. Without a moment's hesitation, he immediately visited the hospital, not as a former colleague, but as a true member of the family, simply to be there with me. In that overwhelming moment, I realized with profound clarity that this is what truly matters at the end of the day. People remember you for the person you're, for the authentic human connection you forged, and not for the position you once held.

Leadership, in its most profound expression, is not a solitary sprint to a predetermined finish line. It's a sacred relay, a continuous passing of the torch of wisdom, empowerment, and inspiration. What you meticulously build within someone today – the confidence you instill, the skills you cultivate, the values you model – will not only shape their present but will inevitably live on in the way they, in turn, lead, mentor, and inspire others tomorrow. Your influence doesn't end with your tenure; it ripples outwards, touching lives you may never meet, shaping futures you may never see. That, in its breathtaking scope, is your enduring legacy.

So, as you stand at this reflective juncture, or indeed at any point in your leadership journey, permit yourself to ponder these searching questions:

- When the day comes for me to depart from this role, this team, this organization, what scent will linger in the air? What stories will be whispered in the hallways? What will be the most vivid, enduring memories I leave behind in the hearts and minds of those I've led?
- In the final accounting of my leadership, will the scales show that I have lifted, empowered, and celebrated more people than I have merely evaluated or critiqued?
- Have I been a catalyst for the creation of new leaders, individuals emboldened and equipped to carry the torch forward, or have I, perhaps unintentionally, cultivated a cadre of competent but dependent followers?

The truest, most enduring measure of your leadership is not confined to the sum of your achievements during your tenure. It's revealed in the vibrancy, the growth, and the positive momentum that continues, and indeed flourishes, long after you have passed the baton and moved on. It's in the leaders you've nurtured who then go on to nurture others, creating a cascading impact of positive influence.

Let your legacy not be one of fleeting power or transient accolades, but one etched in the indelible ink of love translated into daily action, of unwavering belief in the boundless potential of others, and of the quiet courage to consistently do what is right, especially in the unseen moments. That, and nothing less, is the profound, resonant, and timeless legacy of a true people leader.

> *"Try not to become a person of success, but rather try to become a person of value." – Albert Einstein*

Conclusion: Leadership That Lingers – An Echo in the Human Heart

"People may forget what you said, they may forget what you did – but they will never forget how you made them feel." – Maya Angelou

These profound words from Maya Angelou have, in many ways, been the silent underscore to every chapter, every reflection, every shared insight within these pages. They are the distilled essence of a truth that resonates far beyond the corridors of corporate life, reaching into the very core of our human experience. As we draw this particular exploration to a close, let us not merely summarize, but rather, let us breathe deeply, reflect with intention, and fully embrace the enduring resonance of leadership that truly matters.

The Tapestry We've Woven Together

Over the course of this book, we have journeyed far beyond the conventional landscapes of people management. We embarked on this exploration not to dissect a mere organizational function, but to answer a profound calling – a calling to connect, to nurture, and to elevate the human spirit within the context of shared endeavor. We have ventured into the nuanced terrains where leadership is not a title declared from on high, but a daily practice lived in the quiet integrity of our interactions. We've witnessed how trust, that most precious and fragile of currencies, is not minted in grand pronouncements, but painstakingly accrued in the accumulation of everyday choices, consistent actions, and unwavering reliability.

We've listened to the silence where true growth is often nurtured, away from the spotlight, in the thoughtful pause before feedback, in the patient encouragement of a nascent idea. We have navigated the often uncomfortable yet transformative passages of difficult conversations, recognizing that courage is not the absence of fear, but the commitment to speak truth with compassion, even when our voice trembles. And critically, we have unearthed the understanding that sustainable impact, the kind that ripples outwards and endures, is rarely forged through the assertion of power or authority, but through the quiet strength of authentic presence – a presence that sees, validates, and empowers.

We began with a foundational premise: that to manage people is not to manipulate levers of control, nor to orchestrate a symphony of tasks. It's, at its heart, a deeply human endeavor – an invitation to understand the intricate inner worlds of others, to walk alongside them in their journey of growth, and, in doing so, to contribute to the creation of something far greater, more meaningful, and more enduring than any individual ambition. If you have journeyed with us to this reflective juncture, it signifies more than perseverance. It speaks to a resonance within you, a recognition that this deeper, more conscious iteration of leadership is not just a philosophy, but a path you already walk, or one you're now, with earnest intention, ready to begin. And that inner alignment, that willingness to embrace the profound responsibility and privilege of leading others, matters more profoundly than any strategy or skill.

The Unseen Current: The Power You Steward

In the relentless cadence of deadlines and deliverables, amidst the clamor of escalations and the meticulous scrutiny of status reports, it's easy to overlook the quiet, extraordinary current of influence you command. As a people manager, you're a steward of a remarkable power – not a power over, but a power to. It's the power to gently sculpt an individual's burgeoning confidence, to illuminate pathways within their career they might never have perceived alone, and sometimes, in moments of profound connection, to touch and transform the trajectory of a life.

Consider the ripple effects: one conversation, offered with genuine encouragement and belief, could be the gentle yet decisive nudge that propels someone to apply for a role they had dismissed as beyond their reach, unlocking doors to unforeseen potential. A single, thoughtfully constructed feedback session, delivered with empathy and a focus on development, could unearth a latent strength, a hidden talent they were entirely unaware they possessed, altering their self-perception forever. One quiet moment of shared humanity, of unreserved empathy offered when an individual is navigating the silent storms of personal struggle, could be the anchor that holds them together when they feel they are on the verge of breaking inside.

Leadership, in its most authentic expression, transcends the mere act of being in charge. It's the art of becoming a reliable beacon, a steadfast presence others can lean on, especially when the terrain is treacherous and the way forward is obscured. You're not expected to embody perfection; the illusion of the flawless leader is a heavy and unhelpful burden. You're not required to possess an encyclopedic knowledge of all answers; vulnerability and the courage to say "I don't know, but let's find out together" often build deeper trust than feigned omniscience. But if you commit to showing up with unwavering consistency, to caring with genuine sincerity, and to leading with conscious, reflective intention, you'll inevitably create ripples of positive change that extend far beyond the quantifiable grasp of metrics and spreadsheets. You'll be sowing seeds of trust, resilience, and growth that will blossom in ways you may never fully witness, but whose fragrance will linger long after.

Beyond the Insignia of Titles, Towards a Legacy of Impact

Our societal narratives often conflate leadership with the visible markers of seniority – the grand titles, the corner offices, the hierarchical rungs on a corporate ladder. Yet, the most profoundly impactful leaders, those whose influence echoes in the lives they've touched, are seldom defined by such external trappings. They are, more often than not, the individuals who consistently chose to lift others higher, who prioritized the sometimes uncomfortable path of unwavering honesty over the deceptive comfort of expediency. They are the ones who led not with bluster or demand, but with a quiet, humble strength, their actions underpinned by a deep and unshakeable conviction in the potential of their people.

You may never see your name etched onto a commemorative plaque or illuminated on a wall of honor. But your legacy will be vividly inscribed elsewhere, in far more meaningful chronicles. It will be reflected in the newfound confidence radiating from the team member who, nurtured by your encouragement, finally found the courage to voice their unique perspective. It will shine in the tangible success of the individual you mentored, who now pays that guidance forward, amplifying your impact through their own leadership. It will be woven into the very fabric of the culture you painstakingly shaped – not through hollow slogans posted on walls or performative declarations, but through the consistent, undeniable integrity of your daily actions, your choices, your unspoken commitments.

Your true impact is not measured in the volume of applause or the frequency of public accolades. It's far more profoundly gauged by a different set of indicators: Who flourishes and discovers their own capacity for growth when under your stewardship? Whose potential is unlocked? And, perhaps most tellingly, who genuinely feels the void, the absence of your supportive presence, your guidance, your belief, when you're no longer there? That is the quiet, enduring testament to a leadership that matters.

This, Truly, Is the Work That Weaves Meaning into Our Days

In a world increasingly mesmerized by the allure of instantaneous results, by the relentless pursuit of speed and exponential scale, the deliberate act of slowing down, of pausing to genuinely inquire, "How are you really doing?" can feel almost revolutionary. In a culture that often defaults to rewarding only the visible outcomes, the polished end-products, the conscious choice to acknowledge and validate the unseen effort, the struggle, the learning inherent in the process, becomes a profound act of humanity. In a system that seems perpetually geared towards rushing headlong into the next objective, the willingness to pause, to reflect, to offer unwavering support and to foster collective wisdom, emerges as a true hallmark of enlightened strength.

The path of people management, undertaken with this depth of intention, is seldom the easiest route. It's frequently the invisible one, its most crucial contributions often made behind the scenes, away from the glare of public recognition. It can be the emotionally exhausting one, demanding a constant output of empathy, patience, and resilience. It's often the path paved with fewer immediate thank-yous and a greater share of complex human dilemmas, ethical considerations, and challenging choices.

Yet, it's also, unequivocally, the most deeply meaningful one. Because while intricate systems can be optimized, streamlined, and automated, and while complex processes can be re-engineered and technologically enhanced, the unique, irreplaceable essence of human beings cannot be replicated. Their vast, untapped potential, their silent, unseen pain, their most cherished and fragile dreams – these are not abstract concepts; they are palpable realities. And as their manager, their leader, you're bestowed with the rare and sacred privilege of walking beside them, of bearing witness, of offering guidance and support as they navigate the multifaceted tapestry of their professional and personal lives.

This is not merely a role; it's a profound responsibility and an unparalleled opportunity to contribute to the human story in a lasting way.

When the Wellspring Feels Dry, Remember This Resonance

There will inevitably be days, perhaps even seasons, when the mantle of leadership feels impossibly heavy, undeniably thankless. Days when you'll wrestle with the echoes of your choices, questioning if you did enough, if you did right. Moments when your most sincere efforts seem to vanish into the ether, unnoticed, unacknowledged. Times when, despite your best intentions and most dedicated support, someone you invested in chooses a different path, leaving a pang of disappointment. Occasions when conflict seems to drag on interminably, draining your reserves. And periods when the sheer multiplicity of demands feels overwhelming, threatening to extinguish your inner flame.

In those precise moments of doubt and depletion, I urge you to gently, yet firmly, call yourself back to your originating 'why.' You chose this path not for its promise of ease, but for its profound potential for meaning. You embraced this responsibility to cultivate the growth of others, knowing that in doing so, you too would irrevocably grow. You committed to this journey because your aspiration extended beyond merely managing tasks and orchestrating work-you yearned to positively influence lives, to leave an imprint of encouragement, empowerment, and belief.

This is not a burden to be shouldered with resignation. It's, in truth, a precious gift – a unique vantage point from which to foster human flourishing. And while no leadership journey is ever entirely free of the shadows of doubt or the sting of setback, every single step you take with an open heart, with genuine intention, and with unwavering integrity will leave behind something intangible yet incredibly powerful – a residue of trust, a catalyst for growth, a spark of transformation that continues to glow long after the interaction has passed.

A Final, Heartfelt Invitation to Continue the Unfolding

This book was never intended to be a prescriptive manual, a rigid formula for managing the complexities of human interaction. Because people, in their glorious, frustrating, beautiful diversity, are not formulas to be solved. They are living narratives, unfolding stories-each unique, each possessing chapters of triumph and trial, each longing to be truly seen, deeply heard, and genuinely understood. And you – as a people manager, as a leader, as a fellow human being entrusted with guiding others – are far more than a mere task owner, a deliverer of outcomes, or a tracker of progress. You're a story-shaper, a co-author in the evolving narratives of those you lead.

So, as you step back into the rhythm of your days into the strategic depths of your meetings, the intimate spaces of your one-on-ones, the reflective evaluations of reviews, and the countless small yet significant daily interactions – I invite you to carry these gentle inquiries in your heart:

- Whose story needs to be more fully heard today, beyond the surface-level updates?
- Whose spirit can I intentionally uplift with a word of recognition, an act of belief?
- What subtle messages am I sending about the culture I am co-creating, even, and perhaps especially, in my silence, in my non-verbal cues, in the priorities I visibly champion?
- How can I consistently shift the focus of my leadership from being about 'me' and my achievements, to being about 'us' and our collective growth and well-being?

If even a single, heartfelt answer to these questions inspires you to lead with an incrementally greater degree of intention, empathy, and courage tomorrow than you did today, then this book, and our shared journey within it, will have quietly, yet profoundly, fulfilled its purpose.

Because in the End... It's the Echo of Your Humanity That Remains

Spreadsheets will inevitably be archived, their data fading into the annals of past quarters. Projects, no matter how grand or urgent, will reach their conclusion, replaced by new initiatives. Organizational goals will shift and evolve, responding to the ever-changing tides of the external landscape. These are the transient elements of our professional lives.

But what truly stays behind, what endures long after the deliverables are forgotten and the strategic plans are revised, is the indelible imprint you leave on the human heart. It's how you made people feel about their work, about their capabilities, and, most importantly, about themselves during the time they journeyed alongside you.

Did they feel genuinely seen, acknowledged for their unique contributions and their inherent worth?

Did they experience tangible growth, stretching beyond their perceived limitations because you believed in their potential?

Did they feel a sense of psychological safety, a deep wellspring of trust in your integrity, your fairness, your support?

Did they, through their association with you, become fuller, more confident, more capable versions of themselves?

This is your authentic legacy. Not the milestones achieved, but the lives touched. Not the targets met, but the trust built.

Lead with unwavering honesty, for it builds the only foundation that lasts.

Lead with profound humanity, for it acknowledges the shared journey of all.

Lead with an open and courageous heart, for it's the wellspring of true connection.

Because those leaders who commit to this path, who embrace the messy, beautiful, challenging, and deeply rewarding work of nurturing human potential, may not always be the loudest voices in the room, nor the most conspicuously followed figures. But they are, without exception, the ones who are always, and unequivocally, remembered. Their leadership lingers, an echo in the human heart, inspiring others long after they have moved on, shaping a better future, one interaction, one relationship, one person at a time.

References and Inspirations

The ideas and insights presented in this book have been deeply shaped by the work of numerous authors, researchers, and thought leaders. This section acknowledges the foundational texts, contemporary analyses, and inspiring narratives that have contributed to our understanding of effective people management and personal growth. It's through engaging with these diverse perspectives that we can build a more comprehensive and nuanced approach to leading and influencing others.

1. Anoye, A. B., & Kouamé, J. S. (2018). Leadership Challenges in Virtual Team Environment. International Journal of Scientific & Technology Research, 7(7).
2. Armstrong, M. (2014). Armstrong's Handbook of Human Resource Management Practice (13th ed.). Kogan Page.
3. Bogosian, R., & Rousseau, C. (2017). How and Why Millennials are Shaking Up Organizational Cultures. Rutgers Business Review, 2(3), 386–394. https://rbr.business.rutgers.edu/article/how-and-why-millennials-are-shaking-organizational-cultures
4. Carnegie, D. (1936). How to Win Friends and Influence People. Simon and Schuster.
5. Clear, J. (2018). Atomic Habits: An Easy & Proven Way to Build Good Habits & Break Bad Ones. Avery.
6. Covey, S. R. (1989). The Seven Habits of Highly Effective People. Free Press / Simon & Schuster, Inc.
7. Dutta, A., & Chaudhry, S. (2021). Managing People More Effectively: Challenges and Best Practices. Journal of Management Research and Analysis, 8(1), 1–5.

8. Dweck, C. S. (2006). Mindset: The New Psychology of Success. Random House.

9. Fisher, E., & Gonzales, Y. S. (2013). The ABC Manager-How to Manage People More Effectively in Today's Challenging and Demanding Work Environments. Engineering Management Research, 2(1), 67–78. http://www.ccsenet.org/journal/index.php/emr/article/view/24566

10. Goleman, D. (1995). Emotional Intelligence. Bantam Books.

11. Grant, A. (2013). Give and Take: Why Helping Others Drives Our Success. Penguin.

12. Harvard Business Review. (2017). HBR Manager's Handbook: The 17 Skills Leaders Need to Stand Out. Harvard Business Review Press.

13. Heath, C., & Heath, D. (2010). Switch: How to Change Things When Change is Hard. Broadway Books.

14. Iger, R. (2019). The Ride of a Lifetime: Lessons Learned from 15 Years as CEO of the Walt Disney Company. Random House.

15. Iyer, R. (2021). What the Heck Do I Do with My Life? How to Flourish in Our Turbulent Times. Harper Business.

16. Kahneman, D. (2011). Thinking, Fast and Slow. Farrar, Straus and Giroux.

17. Kishimi, I., & Koga, F. (2018). The Courage to Be Disliked: How to Free Yourself, Change Your Life, and Achieve Real Happiness. Atria Books.

18. Karthikeyan, C. (2017). A Qualitative Study on Managing Millennial Mindsets. International Journal of Innovative Research in Engineering & Management, 4(1), 601–609. https://www.researchgate.net/publication/315993912

19. Khera, S. (1998). You Can Win. Macmillan India Ltd.

20. Knies, E., Leisink, P., & Van Der Schoot, R. (2020). People Management: Developing and Testing a Measurement Scale. International Journal of Human Resource Management, 31(6), 705–737. https://www.tandfonline.com/doi/full/10.1080/09585192.2017.1375963

21. Kotter, J. P. (1996). Leading Change. Harvard Business School Press.

22. Maxwell, C J (2013). The 5 Levels of Leadership. Hachette Book Group Inc.

23. Mehtab, K., Rehman, A. U., Ishfaq, S., & Jamil, R. A. (2017). Virtual Leadership: A Review Paper. Mediterranean Journal of Social Sciences, 8(4 S1).

24. Nadella, S., & Shaw, G. (2017). Hit Refresh: The Quest to Rediscover Microsoft's Soul and Imagine a Better Future for Everyone. Harper Business.

25. Newport, C. (2012). So Good They Can't Ignore You: Why Skills Trump Passion in the Quest for Work You Love. Business Plus.

26. Newport, C. (2016). Deep Work: Rules for Focused Success in a Distracted World. Grand Central Publishing.

27. Newport, C. (2019). Digital Minimalism: Choosing a Focused Life in a Noisy World. Portfolio.

28. Pink, D. H. (2009). Drive: The Surprising Truth About What Motivates Us. Riverhead Books.

29. Pillai, R. (2010). Corporate Chanakya. Jaico Publishing House.

30. Prystupa-Rządca, K., & Latusek-Jurczak, D. (2014). Role of the Virtual Team Leader: Managing Changing Membership in a Team. https://doi.org/10.4324/9781315556215

31. Richardson, R., & Thompson, M. (1999). The Impact of People Management Practices on Business Performance: A Literature Review. Institute of Personnel and Development. https://www.researchgate.net/publication/240314661

32. Sinek, S. (2009). Start with Why: How Great Leaders Inspire Everyone to Take Action. Portfolio.

33. Smith, N. (2021). Stop Overthinking: 23 Techniques to Relieve Stress, Stop Negative Spirals, Declutter Your Mind, and Focus on the Present. Thought Catalog Books.

34. Srivastava, R. (2022). The 10 New Life-Changing Skills: Get Them and Get Ahead. Penguin Random House India.

35. Storm, P. M. (1990). Book Review: Mahfooz A. Ansari: Managing People at Work. Organization Studies, 13(1), 140–144. https://journals.sagepub.com/doi/abs/10.1177/017084069201300118

36. Thompson, C., & Gregory, B. J. (2012). Managing Millennials: A Framework for Improving Attraction, Motivation, and Retention. The Psychologist-Manager Journal, 15(4), 237–246. https://www.researchgate.net/publication/263920409

37. Tovmasyan, G. (2017). The Role of Managers in Organizations: Psychological Aspects. Business Ethics and Leadership, 1(3).

38. University of Virginia HR. (n.d.). The Five Roles of a Supervisor. https://hr.virginia.edu/sites/default/files/PDFs/supervisorfiveroles.pdf

39. IMD Business School. Leadership Reflections: People Management. https://www.imd.org/mp/leadership-reflections/people-management/

40. People Matters. Top CEOs and Their People Management Skills. https://www.peoplematters.in/article/leadership/top-ceos-and-their-people-management-skills-17932

41. Farmers Guardian Insight. FG Insight Intelligence Guide – Managing People. http://www.fginsight.com/AcuCustom/Sitename/DAM/033/FG_Insight_intelligence_guide_-_Managing_People.pdf

42. University Forum for Human Resource Development (UFHRD). (2008). Conference Paper: Khandekar, A. https://www.ufhrd.co.uk/wordpress/wp-content/uploads/2008/06/604khandekar.pdf